I'm Not Single, I Have a Dog

I'm Not Single, I Have a Dog

Dating Tales from the Bark Side

SUSAN HARTZLER

DOGS IN OUR WORLD
Series Editor Brian Patrick Duggan

McFarland & Company, Inc., Publishers
Jefferson, North Carolina

ISBN (print) 978-1-4766-8448-2
ISBN (ebook) 978-1-4766-4303-8

Library of Congress and British Library
cataloguing data are available

Library of Congress Control Number 2021006583

Front cover photograph (Shutterstock / Aleksey Boyko)

Printed in the United States of America

*McFarland & Company, Inc., Publishers
Box 611, Jefferson, North Carolina 28640
www.mcfarlandpub.com*

To the memory of
Berry Berenson Perkins

Acknowledgments

I am deeply grateful to the sister of my soul, Kim Ostrovsky, for loving me unconditionally and encouraging me to finish this book. I owe a debt of gratitude to my friend Catherine Overturf since the first grade, who read every single version of the manuscript throughout the many years it took me to write. Thanks also to McFarland and Brian Patrick Duggan for taking a chance on me.

This book would not have been completed without the sage advice of writing coach extraordinaire Mandy Jackson-Beverly as well as the many teachers I've worked with along the way, including Toni Lopopolo, Rita Wilson and every member of their writing groups, especially Marsha Mauhardt, Toni Guy and Lisa Angle. Michael O'Shea, Maura Kruse Noonan and my buddy Leslie Westbrook have been instrumental in my success as a writer. Thanks also to tech girl supreme Penny Fitzgerald and her mom Kay Fitzgerald-Luthi for their prayers and technical support. I am also profoundly grateful to my grade school guardian angel, Steven Montner, M.D., and my third-grade teacher, Mrs. Ring, who suggested I become a writer when I grew up.

My heartfelt appreciation goes to Gene Johnson, Flavia Potenza, Susan Franzblav and Emilie Hamashi Rayman for believing in me and to my dear friends Maria Miereanu and Brenda Piccirillo for always being there, no matter what. I'm blessed to have amazing friends in my life like Susanne Hayek, sisters Dianna and Catherine Bari, Darcy Brinker and Lance Lombardo who listened, read and offered constructive criticism. In the dog world, my deepest thanks go to Marilyn Bennett, Kirsten Cole, and Pam Marks for showing me the many ways to bond with dogs. And I can't forget to thank Michelle Zahn from LePaws for representing me and my current pack.

I want to acknowledge the members of the Dog Writer's Association of America whose work continues to inspire me and Therapy Dogs International for allowing me and my dogs to practice our

Acknowledgments

life purpose. The children we have met over the years are my daily inspiration.

Special thanks to my goddaughters, Natasha Testa and Lindsay Overturf, both true blessings in my life. And last but not least, I am beyond grateful to Siesta, Blondie, Baldwin, and all my extraordinary dog children for sharing their lives with me.

Table of Contents

Table of Contents

Preface

I've always been a good judge of character—at least when it comes to friends and dogs. Romantic relationships haven't turned out so well. At age sixty, I've learned to accept, even love, my single status, provided I have my good friends and a dog or two by my side. But that's not always been the case.

Back in the 1980s, I found it tough to be a never-married woman approaching her thirties. Well-meaning people would ask time after time why I hadn't settled down and started a family. They still do.

Self-help books imply that being single is synonymous with being a neurotic harpy with impossibly high standards. Reading these best sellers made me feel more desperate. Even worse were all the celebrations I attended for my friends—from bachelorette parties and weddings to baby showers—always as the token wallflower. My own family didn't help, either. Mom and Dad treated me like an incompetent child way into my adulthood. The worst part? I behaved like one.

Newsweek magazine didn't help my anxiety when they published the article "Too Late for Prince Charming?" According to the magazine, single women over forty were more likely to be killed by a terrorist than get married. That thought made me, along with other single women across the country, extremely uncomfortable.

Time and time again, I found myself attracted to the quintessential bad boy, a good-looking guy with charisma oozing from his pores, ready and willing to allow a woman to take care of him financially and emotionally. Can you spell *codependent*?

I'm not alone in my attraction to bad boys. Research shows men who have vain and somewhat, well, psychopathic tendencies usually get more dates than the average guy. What's up with that?

Think about it. Bad boys are often ridiculously good-looking. Their egos won't let them look anything other than their best. A naive girl like me had to learn that a bad boy's good looks and charming ways could

1

quickly wear out. They just can't seem to maintain that mesmerizing first impression. But they're never dull, and in my naivety, I preferred them that way. I liked feeling captivated by my man.

Plus, bad boys know how to have a good time. Sure, they're selfish, rule-breakers, and rebellious, but those negative qualities are what I found attractive. If you do, too, don't delude yourself, as I did, into thinking a sexy bad boy will become a devoted partner and loving father. No way.

Here's the worst part: I found that men who depended on me emotionally, physically, and financially made me feel needed. At first, feeling so needed fortified my self-esteem and eased the abandonment anxiety I'd suffered since childhood. I hadn't figured out yet that my compulsive giving and fixing behaviors went hand in hand with my disappointing and disastrous romantic relationships.

I now know that my giver/fix-it pattern stemmed from being raised in a home where vital and important emotional needs were never acknowledged or adequately responded to by the adults in my life. Caregiving became my way to compensate for that deficit.

Don't get me wrong. All parents fail in some sense. As Mitch Albom so eloquently wrote in his *New York Times* best seller *The Five People You Meet in Heaven*: "All parents damage their children. It cannot be helped." I've never heard of a school or college for parents. Mom and Dad did their best and loved me in their way as much as they knew how. But they raised a confused little kid—me.

The one thing I've never been confused about is my deep love of animals, dogs in particular. That love started with my childhood dog, Siesta. An ugly mutt, Siesta taught me about unconditional love and acceptance. Throughout my childhood, that dog stood by my side, always making everything right in my world.

Siesta's love motivated me to rescue Blondie from the pound, my first pet as an adult. I figured some unconditional dog love would help ease my broken heart after getting dumped ... again ... by yet another Mr. Wrong. I figured loving a dog would take care of my codependent tendencies. After all, a dog would never take advantage of me. My dogs never care if I gained a pound (or ten). They live in the moment and don't judge.

I've found dogs to be great listeners. They force me to be active yet are always up for nap or a cuddle session. But probably the best part of being a dog guardian is that no matter what, my canine family members bring out the best in me.

Preface

I've had to learn the hard way that I can't change anybody but myself. Through years of therapy, I've discovered why I was loser bait and what had made me stay with bad boys for so long. I finally figured out how to put an end to entering and staying in unhealthy relationships. It was tough, but I've learned to embrace the life I have without an emotionally draining man by my side. Here's my story. The human names have been made up to protect the privacy of individuals but the dog names in this book remain the same.

1

Canine Intervention

"Maybe this isn't such a good idea," I said to no one in particular.

I traveled solo, as usual, headed to the West Valley Animal Shelter in Los Angeles, hoping to find love. Not just any kind of love. I needed the unconditional kind like I had as a child with my ugly mutt named Siesta. That dog taught me more about love and acceptance than any of the adults in my life.

Backing out of my driveway, I caught a glimpse of myself in my rearview mirror. I hadn't showered since my latest beau broke up with

Siesta gives me a big kiss (author's photograph).

me. My greasy bangs and long blonde bedhead hair was complemented by bloodshot hazel eyes. They were red from crying.

"God, Susan, you could put a little effort into your appearance before leaving the house."

I looked down at my outfit, an old pair of sweatpants with a coffee-stained t-shirt. "No wonder I'm still single. Who could love this hot mess?" I parked my first-ever brand-new car in the parking lot and moved slowly toward the whimpers and cries that echoed outside the pound.

"I'm just looking." I tried to convince myself, but I knew I would bring a dog home. I needed some unconditional dog love to mend my recently broken heart.

Once inside, I choked back tears. Rows of unwanted dogs waited in cages for their forever families. Rejected, abandoned, and unloved myself, I related to all of them. Last night, I'd found out my latest beau was engaged to someone else.

Besides the shelter being noisy, the rank smell of urine mixed with the copper odor of adrenaline and fear made me want to vomit. Depressing. Not the best place to be after getting dumped.

A golden retriever mix tried his best to cheer me up. He ran to the front of his cage to greet me.

"Aren't you pretty?" I said to the big guy. "Way too pretty for me. You remind me of the jerk I'm trying to forget."

A pit bull mix licked my fingers when I petted him through his cage.

"Hello there, my name is Susan," I said in a sing-song voice. "Maybe you want to go home with me."

He looked away as if to say he was waiting for someone else, not me. Typical guy.

A poodle stood stiff, his hair so matted that his legs could barely move.

"Poor baby. Maybe you're the one for me."

The poodle snarled when I came close to the cage.

"I guess not."

Then I spotted her—a medium-sized, golden-haired girl with thick, fluffy fur, her pointy ears flush against her head, her eyes the color of amber. She lay motionless in the back of the kennel, shaking from head to tail. I froze. I understood how she felt because that was how I'd spent the last twelve hours—curled up, shaking, and alone. I had to resist the urge to crawl in and comfort her.

The other two mutts in her cage ran around like crazy, barking for

A portrait of Blondie in a field of flowers (author's photograph).

my attention. A filthy water bowl spilled all over the cement floor in the mayhem. Dirty water puddled underneath the poor golden dog, but she didn't move.

She looked at me. We locked eyes. Her silent despair spoke louder than the deafening growls, barks, and cries that echoed off the walls.

That's my dog.

According to the shelter's records, her name was Prissy. Her original owner had dropped her off at the shelter, claiming she was allergic to her fur.

Really? You keep a dog for five years and then drop her off at the pound? Didn't the original owner's allergies flare up before then? Some people.

The name Prissy didn't fit her. My girl needed something different for her brand-new life.

Blondie. Perfect.

I named my new dog Blondie after my favorite '70s and '80s rock group. She was a German spitz mix, a working breed that came to

America from Germany in the early 1800s. I figured my German heritage had led her to me. Yes, this was destiny.

After I filled out the necessary paperwork, I guided Blondie out of that nasty place to her new reality—life with me. She pulled me outside; she couldn't wait to get out of that place. Neither could I. My new loyal companion leaped into my shiny gray Ford Mustang and made herself comfortable in the front passenger seat. Blondie riding shotgun felt right. She was my new partner.

At twenty-nine years old, I knew I had a problem when it came to the opposite sex. If one hundred single men stood in front of me, I'd pick the worst possible one. All my past relationships to that point had brought up a feeling of dread early on, like I had to hold my breath while I waited for something to go wrong. And it always did—my latest boyfriend debacle being a perfect example. He'd been engaged to someone else the entire time we dated, if you could call what we did together dating. But now, I had a dog, a companion, someone who wouldn't judge me or use me—taking my precious time or money—someone who would love me, no matter what.

At every red light, I stroked Blondie's head and rubbed behind her ears. I couldn't help myself. I had to touch her. I had a dog, and she had me. Her amber eyes closed for a moment in what looked to me like pleasure and gratitude.

"What a good dog. You're going to have a wonderful life now, I promise."

When the light changed to green, her entire body stiffened. The moment I drove through the crosswalk, she opened her mouth wide and gagged. Nothing came out, but she wretched uncontrollably.

"Oh no! Are you sick?"

I steered over to the curb, hoping to get her out in case she vomited. Before I could get there safely, Blondie puked. Did I mention this was my first new car—ever? The vomit dripped from the passenger seat onto the floor. The awful stuff stuck to her beautiful blonde fur. Of course, I hadn't thought to prepare before bringing a dog into my life, so I had nothing in the car to clean up the mess. Good thing we were almost home.

Blondie seemed perfectly healthy when I pulled into the driveway of my one-bedroom apartment in Beachwood Canyon. She ran up the stairs as if she'd lived there her entire life. I loved my home, especially the view of the medieval-looking castle apartment building across the street; it made me feel like a princess. Ah, if only I could find my prince.

1. Canine Intervention

She followed me up the stairs of her new life. After I cleaned her up, Blondie made herself at home on the tiny balcony that overlooked the castle apartment building across the street. She lay there in the late afternoon sun. From that day on, I left the French doors open to the teeny balcony so she could catch the sun. I figured no one would scale the building to break in.

"Is that your sweet spot?" I placed a bowl of water next to her. "You can relax anywhere you'd like. This is your home now."

After the sun went down, Blondie finally came inside and sniffed around to check out her new digs.

"Come on. Get your butt up here." I patted the couch.

Blondie tilted her head, and her ears perked up, as if she were trying to fathom her inscrutable human.

"What dog doesn't want to cuddle with their owner?"

Blondie stared at me.

"That's all I need right now, another rejection."

I picked her up and set her next to me. "Stay."

Siesta relaxing in the backyard of my childhood home, a ranch style house in the San Fernando Valley suburbs of Los Angeles (author's photograph).

She jumped off.

"Are you afraid to sit on the furniture? Poor baby."

Since she wouldn't join me, I sat on the hardwood floor beside her, kissed the top of her head, and brushed her golden fur with my own brush. Gobs of blonde hair came out in the brush and stuck to my clothes, my rug, my mid-century black couch.

"Oh yeah, dogs shed. I forgot about that."

Of course, when I'd bought the black couch cheap at a church rummage sale, I hadn't considered I'd be the proud owner of a dog with blonde fur.

Blondie scratched with abandon. I gave her one of the cans of dog food I'd picked up but she still seemed hungry. So I pulled out some turkey from my refrigerator.

"Here you go."

She gobbled it down.

"And they have fleas! We have a lot to learn about each other."

When the time came for sleep, it didn't surprise me that Blondie refused to jump on my bed. She acted almost too well trained for me. Still, I had to try. With her, I yearned to re-create the bond I'd had with my childhood dog, Siesta. Supposedly a purebred Chihuahua, Siesta had turned out to be an ugly mutt, looking like a cross between a rat and an opossum, but I loved her anyway. We'd slept back to back every night. Her body had warmed me, and her soft snores had lulled me to sleep.

"You've got to do this for me," I lamented aloud.

Blondie looked up from the floor with those amber eyes. Her unspoken response? No.

I relented and placed one of my pillows on the floor next to my bed. Blondie circled twice, nestled down, let out a sigh, and fell asleep in minutes. I lay wide awake, worried about my dog. I'd hoped caring for her would prevent me from dating unhealthy guys. Had I done the right thing?

2

Angel by My Side

The next morning, Blondie and I headed to my friend Angel's house. Angel, short for Angelica, worked as a freelance fashion writer and held the spot in my heart of number one confidante and best friend.

"I hope she'll approve of you, Blondie," I said out loud to the golden dog. "That's a stupid question. Why wouldn't she? Angel loves dogs. She loves everyone."

Angel Pratt, a true angel here on Earth. Like her name, Angel was intelligent and wise, patient, joyful, and absolutely glorious. Exactly ten years older than me, she even looked angelic with her long blonde hair and striking blue eyes. Angel had the distinction of being one of the first people I knew to get a tattoo. She'd chosen an angel, of course, the little cherub forever on her right shoulder.

My new dog barfed again in my car—this time, right on the center console.

"Not again!"

When we arrived at Angel's Laurel Canyon home, Blondie appeared fully recovered from her barf attacks. Me and my Mustang, not so much. But I didn't care. I already loved that dog. She ran quickly to the front door of Angel's Spanish hacienda, sat, and waited for me to catch up.

"Darling!" Angel opened the front door, stepped out to give me a hug, and almost tripped over my golden dog. "Who is this beautiful creature?"

"I'm pleased to introduce you to my new dog, Blondie."

Right on cue, Angel's pack—her Scottie dog named Hobson and the family pound mutts Charlie and Gregory—ran to the door full speed, barking at me and Blondie. They did the ritual butt sniff, circling each other.

"Oh, darling, she's beautiful. Where did Blondie come from?" Angel bent down to pet Blondie. Luckily, my new dog didn't have any barf on her head.

"I broke her out of the pound yesterday. Be careful. She threw up all over my new car."

"A little throw-up won't hurt your car. Oh, darling, I'm so glad. Rescue dogs are the best. They're so grateful to be out of their cages."

"Grateful, yes, but I'm afraid she's sick or something. I didn't even consider that possibility."

"She looks healthy to me. Probably not used to car rides. Right, Blondie?"

Blondie followed Angel into the kitchen like she belonged there. Angel gave me a wet cloth and some cleaning spray.

"Here, you clean your car, and I'll take care of your precious girl."

After I wiped up all the barf, I went back in the house to see Angel surrounded by all four dogs. Angel couldn't help but mother everyone, even my golden mutt and especially me.

"She's fine. Look at her eat up this turkey."

My heart swelled. Blondie was already part of the pack.

"Still, I'd have her checked by a vet. They'll tell you if something's wrong. Do you have a vet?"

"The shelter gave me the name of one." I fumbled around in my purse for the info.

"Our vet is fabulous. Call mine instead. I'll give you his number. He'll take care of you and little Miss Blondie. Did the shelter give you any food for her?"

"I picked up a few cans on the way home. What should I feed her anyway?"

Angel pulled a large bag out of her cupboard. I assumed she would pour some out for me to take home. But not Angel.

"Here, take this bag of kibble home with you."

All four dogs stood at attention, hoping to get into the bag of food.

"No, guys, this is for Blondie," Angel told the canine gang. "Now, you're sure you can have a dog where you live?"

"Oh no. I didn't even think to ask my landlord. You think it'll be okay?"

"How could anyone refuse you and this beautiful creature?"

Angel looked like a woman on a mission. She opened her kitchen cabinets and pulled out everything I needed for my new dog, placing it in a pile by the front door. I left with food and water bowls, dog toys, grooming supplies, a leash, and even a swanky pink rhinestone collar.

"Don't forget this." Angel put a dog bed on top of the growing pile.

Blondie jumped, startled by the teakettle.

"Don't be scared," I told my golden dog. "I'm your new mommy, and I'm here to take care of you."

Angel gave me a cup of tea, and I followed her into the dining room. I took my normal place at the long, rustic dining room table. All four dogs settled underneath, their bellies full of turkey.

"As usual, I didn't think this through. Thank God for you. Otherwise, this dog wouldn't have anything she needs."

"Don't be so hard on yourself, darling," Angel said. "You are a very capable young lady."

"Capable? Ha," I said. "Who doesn't get prepared before they bring a dog home? The same person who jumps into relationships without any thought. You know that guy Dave I've been seeing for the past six months? He's been engaged to someone else this whole time."

Angel had listened to my whines and complaints many times before; my search for a husband to love consumed me.

"Now, Blondie makes sense; she'll be faithful and give you someone to care for," Angel consoled me.

"I guess a rebound dog's better than a rebound man," I said, "but I'm not even sure she likes me."

"What makes you say that?"

"I don't know. She acts aloof, like she rescued me, not vice versa."

Blondie touched my leg with her wet nose and then headed under the table.

"Oh, sweetikins, you've got to give her a little time. Imagine how you'd feel after being behind bars at the shelter."

Content and happy with her life, Angel had tied the knot years before with actor John Pratt, and they'd welcomed two daughters, Percy—short for Priscilla—and Presley. Angel *loved* Elvis Presley.

"I gave Dave enough time, thought for sure he loved me. We'd cuddle for hours after making love, like we were a real couple. But he never spent the night."

To me, Angel had the family, the loving marriage, and the perfect life I yearned for. If only her luck would rub off on me, especially in the romance department. I hadn't reached the age of thirty yet, so I had plenty of time to find my soulmate, get married, and start a family. Even so, I still felt anxious that it would never happen for me.

"I had a boyfriend like that once, a real player," Angel said as she took a sip of her tea with no pretense, no raised pinkie, although she could have behaved entitled with her British pedigree. "The bastard broke my heart. We've all got to learn."

Angel had grown up in London and attended boarding school in Switzerland. Me? I had grown up in the San Fernando Valley and been active in the Girl Scouts. Her father was a diplomat, her mother a socialite. My dad, Richard, worked as an engineer, mom, Margaret, a first-grade teacher. Angel's family was friends with the royal family, and mine were members of the local United Methodist Church.

"When will I learn? I should've known Dave wanted a quick booty call." A chill ran down my spine. I allowed the tea to warm my insides. "Why else would he ring my doorbell at midnight? Duh! He never invited me out after his night shift as a chef, never wanted to go anywhere with me when I asked. Once again, I denied the obvious."

"Oh, Susan, darling girl, I wish I knew how to make you feel better," Angel said. She peeked at my dog under the table. "But I'm sure this dog will help. Look at her, already lying at your feet."

"She is?" I looked under the table too.

"She'll love you unconditionally, she'll give you something to care about, and she might even keep you from dating these losers."

Blondie looked back at me with her amber eyes.

"From your mouth to God's ears," I said, crossing myself.

"You know what they say. The best way to get a man is to stop searching for love. Put the idea right out of your pretty little head, darling."

"You're right. I do tend to obsess. Now, I can fixate on my dog. I've wanted a dog of my own for years, but my parents always talked me out of it. They think of me as their baby, an irresponsible mess. Both Mom and Dad lecture me all the time to get married first, have babies, and then get a family dog."

"That nonsense is shoved down every little girl's throat." Angel stood up and motioned with her teacup that she needed a refill.

"Yes, it is," I answered.

"Look, parents can be too judgmental, sweetikins."

"Mine definitely."

"Darling, you're a responsible young lady, capable of caring for a dog."

"You're right; I can do this." I slapped the table. "As a kid, I took care of all sorts of pets, even nursed injured birds back to health. Once I rescued a dove right out of my own cat's mouth. I didn't have a clue how to care for those injured birds. I just knew I had to care for them."

Angel poured more hot water into my cup. "See? You're a regular Dr. Doolittle."

"Yes, I guess I am." I laughed in agreement.

2. Angel by My Side

"You take such good care of our dogs. I trust you more than anyone with Percy and Presley. Who knows? You might meet the man of your dreams at the dog park. Sweetikins, what a brilliant idea."

* * *

On the way home from Angel's, I thought about all those birds I'd nursed back to health and watched fly away. I found them everywhere. Caring for those birds had given me such a sense of satisfaction. Those birds had needed me, and that'd felt good. At that moment, I realized that I'd been searching to re-create that feeling as an adult by saving wounded birds in the form of men. I dated them, took care of them, believed I could nurture them to health, and then we'd fly off into the sunset together. I figured those damaged men would never leave me. Instead, they'd owe their new, healthy life to me, and we'd start a family and live happily ever after—or so I imagined.

Being the youngest in a family of three kids, I felt useless, pushed aside by my older and wiser siblings. I worried about being the stupid one in my family. Erin and Will knew everything; I'd never catch up. Listening to Mom talk about her kids to friends and family over the phone only reinforced my fears.

"*Erin is going to be a doctor when she graduates from UCLA,*" Mom said in her low, raspy voice. "*Will is a financial genius,*" she cooed. "*Susan, well, we expect her to marry well.*" Mom's voice sounded like she'd smoked too many cigarettes in her life, which she had.

I believed her. Everyone did. I looked up to Erin and Will. I wanted to be just like them someday. But I would never catch up. I'd always be treated like the baby of the family, no matter what I accomplished. But I wouldn't let them, or anyone, deter me. I'd make it to the altar; I had to. Maybe rescuing Blondie would be the first step.

3

Speed Dating
at the Veterinary Hospital

On the way to her vet appointment, Blondie threw up again in my car. Cleaning up her vomit had become a habit, one I didn't particularly like. But I'd learned my lesson and prepared for the inevitable with towels and cleaning supplies for both dog and car.

The veterinary hospital looked like something you'd find in a small town, not one you'd expect in the heart of Los Angeles. The packed waiting room made me feel confident that I'd come to the right place.

"I'm sorry, girl, but you've got to see the doctor."

Blondie refused to enter the office, pulling so hard at the end of her leash that her pink rhinestone collar came off. She headed back to the car in a hurry, but I caught her and picked her up.

"You're not getting out of this. Sorry." I carried her in my arms.

Everyone in the waiting room stared at my trembling pup. I spotted an empty seat right next to a good-looking guy around my age, sitting with his well-behaved Labrador retriever puppy, wearing a Future Guide Dog vest.

The lab puppy had the same chocolate-colored hair and deep brown eyes as his owner. Just my type—tall and lanky—the man, not the dog, although he was pretty cute too. The fact that he was training a guide dog made him even more attractive to me. Perhaps Blondie would lead me to my soulmate, like Angel had predicted.

"Looks like someone doesn't like the vet," the future guide-dog owner said.

"I think she's sick." I tried to stay calm and let him know my interest through eye contact. Impossible with a forty-pound shaking dog mess in my arms.

The front door opened, and another good-looking guy entered. This one was big and beefy, like a Rottweiler.

My eyes traced his triceps and biceps. I felt my heart begin to race.

16

3. *Speed Dating at the Veterinary Hospital*

The lab puppy went crazy the closer he came. I went crazy too, especially when I noticed he didn't have a ring on the finger of his well-manicured left hand. A bodybuilder. Not my usual type, but what the heck? He could offer me the encouragement I needed to go to the gym. I started daydreaming about working out with him until he planted a big kiss on the lips of the future guide-dog owner.

"Honey, look at this dog from the pound." The future guide-dog owner pulled a treat out of his pocket and held the bribe for Blondie.

"I don't think she'll eat anything," I said. "She's been throwing up."

She took it right away.

"Treats can cure any bellyache," the hunk said. "Besides, dogs throw up for a number of reasons."

She grabbed another treat and inhaled it. "She likes turkey," he said, pulling another morsel out for her. I tried not to look deflated. Just my luck, these two were a couple. And a happy couple too. At least I could pick their brains. They must know a lot about dogs, training a service dog and all.

"Do you think she has parvo?"

"No. I've seen dogs with parvo," Hunk said. "She looks healthy to me. She's just scared. Bring treats with you next time she has to go to the vet. She'll get over her fear."

"You think so?"

"No question about it," Hunk's partner, the future guide-dog owner, added. He gave her one more treat before the three of them were called into the exam room.

A mother and her two sons entered the office with their big, fluffy, older golden retriever. The boys played with tiny toy cars, running them on an invisible racetrack all over their dog. The dog didn't mind. In fact, it looked happy and content.

"That could be us one day."

"Blondie?" The receptionist woke me from my daydream. It was time to see the doctor.

"Who do we have here?" The examination room smelled sterile, but Dr. Winters made me feel all warm inside. He didn't look like a typical doctor in his Western jeans and polo shirt. The handsome, rugged man made my heart shake in rhythm with Blondie's entire body.

"My dog's sick. I think she got something serious from the pound."

"Let's take a look."

He carefully took Blondie from my arms but didn't put her on the cold metal table like I'd assumed he would. Instead, Dr. Winters gently placed her on the floor and knelt down to examine her. I liked that.

"Have you seen a dog shake like this? I'm afraid she's having a heart attack."

"A heart attack's not likely," Dr. Winters said. "If she had some genetic predisposition or specific medical factor, then I might worry about that."

"I don't know anything about her health history." My fear over Blondie's health eased, replaced by excitement over this handsome vet.

He warmed the stethoscope in the palm of his hand before placing it on her. "Her heart's strong."

I imagined those hands on me.

"Thank God," I said while I touched his shoulder.

"Why do you think she's sick?" he asked in his deep, velvety voice.

"Sh-she-she keeps throwing up." I couldn't speak with this handsome vet in front of me.

"How many times has she thrown up?" He turned his full attention away from my dog and moved close to me, intensely looking at me.

"Ev-ev-every time she rides in my car."

"She gets car sick. That's common."

"Really?" I sighed with relief, wanting to kiss him right there.

Kneeling again, he took a look inside Blondie's mouth, felt her gums, examined her teeth. "I'd say she's about five years old."

She didn't struggle at all during the exam, seemingly comfortable in his hands. Those hands were big and strong with jagged fingernails.

He's a real man, I thought. That was when I noticed the wedding band. *Darn ... a real man who's really married.*

"I'll give you a prescription for antinausea. You'll need to give her a tablet about an hour before you take her in the car. She should get used to car rides in about a week."

I followed the married vet's directions.

A few car rides on antinausea medicine, and *voilà*, Blondie became a real car riding pro. In time, she even stuck her head out the window, her golden fur flying. Too bad this handsome vet didn't have the cure to my lovesickness too.

4

Think Pawsitive

I spotted Angel at the crowded restaurant and weaved my way through the Hollywood elite who ate breakfast at Hugo's every morning. You never knew who you'd see there. But that day, I didn't care about stargazing. I couldn't wait to see my BFF.

The restaurant looked like an upscale diner, only with crisp white table linens, giving it a chic and clean look. This was the place where many movie deals were made. Nothing fancy, but the location worked for both of us and they knew what Angel liked. I liked the natural light that streamed through the floor-to-ceiling windows.

The two of us dined at the industry hot spot at least once a week. Afterward, I'd head to my office in Beverly Hills. Angel worked freelance so she set her own schedule—lucky girl. Another thing I admired about her.

"Excuse me, miss."

I avoided bumping into a waiter, who held a tray of food and hot coffee.

"Jeez, I'm sorry." When I turned around, I noticed the waiter's adorable dimples.

He held my gaze and that heavy tray for a few more seconds than normal. I didn't mind—until I remembered the chef I'd dated. Crazy hours, drinking on the job, too much partying. Lesson learned.

I noticed Angel sipping her coffee, waiting for me at our usual table in the center of the restaurant. Oh, how she loved her coffee with a smidgen of cream. No artificial flavors for Angel.

"You were so right," I said. "As usual."

Angel and I did the obligatory LA air kiss before I sat down across from her.

"Blondie is better than Prozac. She does this happy dance every day when I get home from work, and it makes me feel so loved."

"Dogs are known for being natural mood boosters; that's why

they're referred to as man's—or, in this case, woman's—best friend."
Angel winked and then took off her suede jacket, the one with the fringe.

I wanted that jacket. With her own fashion sense, no matter what she wore, Angel looked like she'd stepped out of a magazine in her own unique, quirky way.

"I've been feeling more optimistic about life, that's for sure," I said, and I meant it. "Who cares that I'm not married yet?"

"That's brilliant, darling."

Our waiter, the same guy I'd almost collided with, interrupted us. "How are you two beautiful ladies this morning?" He pulled up a chair as if he were joining us for a meal. "What can I get you?" Mr. Dimples gave me that look—the one that said he'd like my phone number.

"I'll have scrambled eggs with a side of broccoli," Angel said. She followed a strict diet and exercised regularly.

"I'll have the same." I preferred some chocolatey morsel to almost anything on any menu but tried to copy my friend and embrace a healthy lifestyle—at least whenever we were together.

"You look familiar," Mr. Dimples said to me.

I felt my face flush.

"Oh, I get that all the time," I said. "Must have a familiar-looking face."

Angel looked at me and then at the waiter. She broke out in a grin that would have made the Cheshire Cat jealous.

"All right, then. Two healthy breakfasts coming up." Mr. Dimples stood and walked toward the kitchen.

"I think he likes you," Angel said.

"He's a waiter," I said, "an out-of-work actor. Not marriage material."

"But the attention makes me feel hopeful," I added. "And he is pretty cute."

"Love is everywhere, darling," Angel said. "You've just got to open your eyes."

"I know. Time to change my stinkin' thinkin.'"

"I've noticed when I look at the bright side of life, positive things happen—*always*," Angel said, her hands around her coffee cup. "It's certainly a state of mind worth developing."

I nodded and asked, "How do you stay so positive? I mean, you didn't even complain about breaking your elbow last year."

"That was a really bad week, remember?" Angel looked off in the distance, and her smile disappeared. "It all started when I found the girls' bunnies drowned in the pool after someone left the door to their hutch open."

"I remember. That was a horrible morning."

"Thank God you came to my rescue. I had to get those bunnies out of there before the kids came home from school."

"Didn't someone steal your '57 Chevy that week too?"

She took a deep sigh. "I really loved that car."

"I know; it was a great car, one of a kind, like you. The silver lining is your brand-new BMW." *Look at me, seeing the glass half full instead of empty. I could get used to this positive attitude.*

We were interrupted again by Mr. Dimples.

"Here you go." He set our plates in front of us. "*Bon appétit*, ladies. *Ciao.*" He gently touched me on the shoulder before heading to the next table.

"Maybe just a fling?" I suggested, my stomach fluttering. "Please?"

"That's what you said last time, darling," Angel reminded me. She reached across the table and took my hand in hers. "I don't want you to get hurt again."

A gold hunk of a ring with a simple cross on it blinded me when it hit the ray of sunlight that streamed through the restaurant's windows.

"Wait a minute. Where'd you get that ring?"

Hard to believe I noticed any specific piece of jewelry Angel wore. She layered her jewelry on thick. Bracelets stacked on her wrists, her chest dripping in necklaces. Not all gold and silver pieces, either, although they could have been. Precious, semiprecious, simple bead-work—she wore it all at once, and it made sense on her.

"John had this made for me for my birthday." She took the ring off and handed it to me. "It came a little late, but I love it."

"See," I said. "That's what I need." I slipped the ring on my engagement finger. "Someone like your John."

"He's come a long way in the gift department. He used to give me cookware or appliances as presents. You know, things like pots and pans. They were all top of the line, but the year I got a vacuum cleaner for Christmas, I realized I had to train him in the fine art of gift-giving."

"And he listened to you? That's impressive."

"True. No relationship is perfect," Angel said. "But John is a sweetheart. He's the kindest man I've ever known and such a brilliant father. That's what you deserve."

"You're right. I might not be perfect, but I have a good heart."

"Any man would be lucky to have you by his side." Angel looked me in the eyes. "My wish is for you to find a love like the man I married."

"How did you meet John?" I asked.

"I never told you?"

I shook my head.

"Our love story began when I was in the fifth grade at boarding school." She pushed her bangs out of her face. "I developed a crush on a certain handsome American actor. I even kept a scrapbook filled with press clippings and photos of him."

"Really?" I asked. "You knew him back then?"

She nodded, and her cheeky grin returned. "Knew *about* him. Everyone did. His career and life were topics of the tabloids. The heart-throb became my teenage crush."

"I know what that's like," I said. "Jackson Browne stole my teenage heart. I did get backstage at one of his concerts and told him I loved him. He didn't respond."

She twirled her wedding ring—white gold with a raw piece of turquoise. "I had no idea I'd ever meet John, let alone marry him."

"Only you would get to marry your teenage crush."

"John lived in New York, so when I moved there, I put the word out that I wanted an introduction." She gazed at her wedding ring. "At the same time, *Vogue* magazine was doing a story on my family. John saw that article with the family photos and told his friends he'd found the perfect woman—me! The whole thing was magical."

"Unbelievable," I said. "Like a fairy tale. Go on..."

"Felt like one too. Still does." Angel's eyes sparkled. "I heard he'd RSVP'd to a party in a Park Avenue penthouse and got myself invited. After about five minutes, guess who walked in? The moment we met, I knew my life was about to change. I never looked back."

"Maybe I should start a scrapbook."

"I don't know about that," she said. "Maybe you need to stop obsessing."

"You're right. Think positive. Live in the moment, just like Blondie does."

"That's a good idea, but you can't give up completely." Angel's forehead creased. "You've got to give your dreams some of your attention. The key to life is balance."

"Okay, so how do I attain balance?"

"Buddha said, 'Maintain a state of balance between physical acts and inner serenity, like a lute whose strings are finely tuned.'"

"I like that, never heard it before."

"Why don't you create a vision board?"

"Never heard of that, either," I answered.

"Everyone's making them," she said. "A vision board is filled with images that represent whatever you want to be, do, or have in your life. You know, cut pictures or quotes you like out of magazines."

"Sounds like fun," I said, imagining what I would add to mine.

"Let's do it together," Angel suggested. "You could make yours all about your perfect man, what he looks like, what he acts like, what your life together will be like. Envision the whole romance."

"I've written about my future hubby," I said, "but I've never done anything like a vision board. Can't hurt."

"Have fun with it," she said.

"I don't get it. I'm in control of other parts of my life. I love my job and have amazing friends, like you. So much for my new, positive attitude, Ms. Buddha."

"You've got to be grateful."

"I am grateful, but I'm also pissed off." I crossed my arms. "No matter how much I try, I can't fix the one thing that bothers me most. I can't find my Mr. Right."

"You could meet your true soulmate tomorrow." She rested her chin on her hands.

"Speaking of soulmate, I'm the maid of honor at yet another wedding this month. That's the fourth this year."

"See? Everyone loves you. The real question is, do you love yourself?"

"At least enough to be in their weddings. I'd love myself a whole lot more if I stopped dating Mr. Wrong or his awful twin brother over and over again."

"Stop fixating on your past failures and disappointments," she said. "Believe that love will come your way."

"I guess you're right again." I soaked up the last of my eggs with a piece of toast.

"Concentrate your energies on staying positive. Picture in your mind exactly the man you'd like, and you watch. He'll come along when you least expect him."

"I'll try," I said, pushing my plate away. "But I'm afraid I'll end up with a loser—or worse, alone."

"Lots of losers in this town," she said. "Like vampires, they suck the life out of you."

"Tell me about it. I've dated all of them."

Angel finished her breakfast and sat back in her chair, eyebrows raised. "Can't you stay away from them?"

23

"It's just that I seem to be attracted to such needy men," I said. "Like the wounded birds I used to nurse back to health when I was a kid."

"It's easy to mistake the feeling of familiarity with love," Angel counseled. "You've become familiar, comfortable with needy men. You've got to change that."

"I'm only trying to help them grow into the partner I know they could become," I said, my shoulders dropped. "You admitted you had to train John. Why is my situation so different?"

"Letting another person know what you need from them is different than needing to change another person."

"I guess so." I slumped back in my chair.

I heard what she'd said, but I still didn't have a clue when it came to healthy relationships.

"Hey, don't frown," she said. "What happened to that positive attitude you had moments ago?"

5

Growing Up Dog Weird

"Blondie, we've been together for a week now. Time to introduce you to the parents."

My golden dog curled up in the passenger seat.

"Don't throw up, okay? You need to make a good first impression."

Mom, a first-grade teacher, and Dad, an engineer, had purchased the three-bedroom, ranch-style tract home in a suburb of Los Angeles, the San Fernando Valley. They purchased it in the early '60s for $33,000. Today, that home is worth in excess of $800,000. It is surrounded by mountains, and many families, including mine, had moved there for the exceptionally good schools. That made the valley an idyllic place to grow up, as long as your parents didn't act like misplaced Quakers like mine had.

I felt a pit in my stomach, driving the 405 freeway. Not because of the traffic. I worried about admitting to Mom and Dad that I had gotten a dog.

"I don't care what they say." I patted Blondie on the head. "I'm not taking you back to that filthy pound. No way."

I remembered the handsome Dalmatian named Pepper—the family dog before Siesta. The spotted puppy had come with an impeccable pedigree, but Mom and Dad hadn't even attempted to train him. I guessed they'd expected him to figure out how to behave properly on his own. He didn't. His powerful frame knocked my little friends off their feet, and me too.

If Mom and Dad had done their due diligence and researched the breed, they would have known that Pepper was not a good match for us. Dalmatians need a strong leader. Our family leader, Dad, preferred his office to our home. Mom had her hands full with three kids, all under the age of ten.

Whenever Pepper did anything wrong, which happened often, Mom and Dad would yell at the poor dog. Even as a child, I had seen how all that shouting made Pepper nervous.

Today, I know that dogs needed direction and consistency, like kids. My parents had raised me and my siblings, Erin and Will, the same way they raised pets. Ignorant dog owners, ignorant parents.

When they'd had enough of his destructive ways, Mom and Dad had sent Pepper away to a ranch. At least, that was what they'd told me. I had grown up afraid they'd send me away, too, if I did anything that might scar their reputation as pillars in the community. And for good reason.

"I'm going to ship you off to your uncle in New York," Mom would say when I misbehaved. "See how you like that!"

* * *

The sweet scent of citrus blossoms from the Valley's orange groves welcomed me home. Blondie smelled good too. I'd given her a bath that morning in preparation for the big introduction.

Mom's New England heritage influenced her decorating style. Still, most of the furniture was secondhand, picked up at yard sales. Like mother, like daughter. Only she could afford new. Even the off-limits formal living room's emerald-green velvet couch came to us compliments of our next-door neighbor. I remembered helping Will lug it over to our house.

"Looks brand-new," Mom had said with pride.

That couch hadn't gone very well with our blue shag carpet, but she'd liked it.

She'd acted like we were the poorest family on the block, but we weren't. The Hartzler residence didn't have a pool like almost every other home in the valley. We were the last to get a color television set too. Dad took the bus to work, and Mom drove the family car—a '56 Ford—well into the '70s. She chauffeured me and my little friends to grammar school every day.

"Bus stop, bus stop, Dearborn Street School," she'd say while she pumped the brakes. "Lean to the front of the bus."

Her antics had made us all giggle in the backseat.

Eclectic doesn't begin to describe her.

I took a deep breath, trying to steady myself before entering the back door. Mom sat in the den, the only light coming from a secondhand table lamp.

"What's that?" She pointed at Blondie without looking up from her book.

"A dog, Mom. I'm taking care of her for a friend," I said and plopped down on the red leather chair across from her. Once again, fear of being shipped away had stopped me from telling the truth.

Getting her approval back then had seemed like the most important thing in my life. Truth was, I felt stuck as their little girl in a woman's body. I had become a model prisoner, an expert at pleasing everyone but myself.

* * *

On the way home, I tried to figure out why I'd fibbed about Blondie. My dishonesty brought me back to my teenage years when Mom and Dad had caught me lying by omission, thanks to a new bedspread with a matching dust ruffle. That was how Mom had found my private journal hidden between the mattress and box frame. I'd been writing in journals for years by then, and I'd had a stack in my closet that she never read, as far as I knew.

But my latest journal was different.

I admitted everything in that journal. I'd smoked cigarettes, drunk beer, and slept next to a boy, and I wrote about my experiences ... in great detail ... with the sensibility of a sixteen-year-old with raging hormones.

That Saturday afternoon, I came home from a fun day spent at a neighbor's pool to my angry mom waiting for me at the back door.

"I read it!" Mom said, arms crossed, red-faced, enraged.

I knew what those three little words meant. She'd read my diary.

Before I launched into my defense or argued about my journal being sacred and personal, Mom threw up her hands and ran through the house, her pretty, flowered muumuu flailing.

"Oh my God, not my daughter, no!" she screamed. "Why, oh why? What did I do wrong?"

I wanted to run, too, wanted to yell back, but I couldn't move.

Mom stopped directly in front of me and stared me down. "Go to your room. We'll see what your father has to say about this, young lady."

Shit-shocked like never before, I grabbed Siesta and headed to my room. That was when I saw the brand-new bright yellow polka-dotted comforter with matching dust ruffle.

"That damn dust ruffle," I told Siesta. "I hate it." I ran my fingernails over the comforter, wanting to rip it to shreds. "My life is over, Siesta."

I listened to the sweet sound of a woodpecker busy in the tree outside my room, something that always put me in a good mood. Not this time.

Mom abruptly entered. "We're having a family meeting tonight when your father gets home. Don't think those tears will get you out of this.

You'll tell him everything I read in your diary. I mean, everything." She slammed the door.

We'd never had a family meeting before. I had no idea what to expect, except the worst.

The family meeting took place in our formal living room—the first time we gathered together there as a family without company. Mom seated me in a chair across from Dad. I could barely look at him. Mom, Erin, and Will sat across from us on the green velvet couch. At least they let me hold Siesta in my lap.

"Go ahead," Mom said. "Tell him."

"I drank a beer." I hugged Siesta, tearing up.

Dad's forehead creased, and he shook his head. I wasn't that surprised. Mom and Dad were teetotalers and then some.

"I only tasted it," I said. "Didn't like it."

"Go on," Mom said.

"I tried a cigarette; it made me dizzy."

"What's wrong with you?" Dad's rosy cheeks turned white. "We taught you better than that."

"That's not all," Mom said, hovering over me. "Is it, Susan?"

"I kissed a guy," I sheepishly admitted. "No big deal."

"An older boy," Mom added. "She slept with him, too, didn't you, Susan Frances?"

Never a good thing when she used my middle name too.

"Planned to run off with him. Tell him, Susan."

I felt her eyes burning my soul.

"I slept next to him." I tried to reason. "In my own sleeping bag. And in my defense, I didn't run away with him. I'm still here."

Dad turned away from me. "You make me sick." His words were a low blow to my already aching ego.

All this over a lie I hadn't even made.

"What do you think of your sister's behavior?" Mom snapped at Erin.

"I think she needs to get on birth control," Erin answered.

Mom's nostrils flared, and her eyes protruded. "That's not very helpful." Putting her youngest on birth control was not something Mom wanted to even consider.

"I wanna hang out with her," Will added. "Sounds like she's having fun."

I still loved my brother for sticking up for me. And his opinion held weight. He held the position of favorite in Mom's heart.

"That's enough," Mom scolded everyone but Dad.

5. Growing Up Dog Weird

"You're grounded," Dad announced. Before that day, none of us kids had ever been grounded. "Get out of here. I can't stand looking at you."

Up until that moment, I'd held the position as Daddy's little girl. That day, I fell off my pedestal, never to return.

"We're keeping an eye on you," Mom said. "No going out with your friends, no parties, no phone calls, no nothing. You're grounded until you turn eighteen."

Grounded for two years?

I tossed and turned that night, worried and angry. Mom had read my diary. How unfair. Did my parents even love me? I didn't think so.

At two in the morning, I crept out of bed, grabbed all my journals, and headed for the backyard. Siesta followed, yawing. Since our home sat on a half-acre, I knew how to stay hidden, and my parents wouldn't wake.

Siesta stood by my side under the crepe myrtle tree and watched me dig a hole deep enough to fit all my journals, the ones I'd written since I was a little girl.

Later, I learned that the drought-resistant crepe myrtle was known as the carefree tree, a fitting place to free myself of my past.

Mom would never read about my deepest feelings ever again.

I poured lighter fluid on the stack and struck a match. The journals twisted into ash, and the words on the pages disappeared in flames. Yesterday up in smoke, dead and gone.

The memory of my teenage years haunted me the following Saturday. I'd finally built up the courage to tell my parents the truth about Blondie. I'd do almost anything to avoid their wrath, but I needed to come clean.

"I'm here," I said, entering the back door with my dog in tow. "I brought lunch, your favorite submarine sandwiches." My hope? To butter them up before making my big announcement.

"That dog is still with you?" Mom asked.

"Yes," I admitted, setting TV trays in the den.

We had eaten on those damn trays throughout my childhood. So much for the family meal.

"I wanted to talk to you about that," I sheepishly said.

"Listen, that'd better not be your dog," Mom warned me.

"Well, you better get used to her. She is mine."

"We don't need any more pets around here," she said. "That cat you gave your father is enough. He keeps biting and scratching us." Mom held out her arm, covered in gashes from the cat's sharp claws.

"Oh my God, you can't have a pet that hurts you like that. Let me find Terry a new home."

"No! We love that cat. He's a real character. Your father buys him fresh turkey; he'll only eat it if it's fresh. Watch this. He talks to us. Here, kitty, kitty."

Right on cue, the big tomcat swaggered into the room and let out a low, guttural growl, his tail stiff, ears back, ready to fight. Hard to remember this gray brute as the cute and cuddly kitten I'd found, abandoned.

The bully cat headed straight for Blondie, back arched, hackles up. Blondie took one look at the angry cat and jumped in my lap for protection.

"No, you don't!" I shooed Terry away from my golden dog.

Terry turned away and then jumped on the couch and seated himself on the armrest next to Mom.

"You don't need a dog," Dad said. "Who's going to train it?"

I wanted to scream at him for his hypocrisy, but I kept my mouth shut. "It's a she, Dad," I said. "And she's already five years old, so she doesn't need any training."

"Come on, Susie," Dad said. "You need a husband, not a dog. Besides, you've got to concentrate on your full-time job, not a pet."

"Dogs sleep a lot. She's fine staying home while I'm at the office."

"Listen, don't ask us for money," Mom added. "Pets are expensive. You'll be surprised at how much it costs to take her to the vet, let alone buy food and pay for everything that goes along with owning a dog."

My parents didn't know how to handle their pets, not Pepper or Terry the cat, let alone their three children. Time for me to grow up and give myself approval.

*   *   *

Night after night, Blondie chose to sleep in the dog bed Angel had given her instead of next to me. But after coming clean with my parents, I needed her more than ever.

"Blondie, come here." I patted my bed once again.

Somehow, she understood what I wanted this time, ran toward me, flew through the air, and landed on the bed.

"Good girl!"

My golden dog lathered me with wet, sloppy dog kisses before finding her sweet spot at the foot of my bed. Her rhythmic breathing lulled me to sleep. I felt safer and more secure than I had in a long time. I might not have found a man, but I'd found my dog.

6

Love Quest

I'd never been a morning person. When I had been young, Mom found it amusing to get my butt out of bed every morning with the gospel song "Rise and Shine," singing at the top of her lungs in her raspy voice while banging a tambourine. I'd jump out of bed, startled, my heart racing. In contrast, waking up to the sight of Blondie sent a tingling warmth radiating through my entire body. I'd open my eyes to my furry alarm clock and realize how lucky I was.

Every day began with Blondie eagerly following me into the kitchen, hungry for her breakfast. I'd pull the bag of kibble out of my cupboard and watch Blondie break out in her happy dance.

"How are you so blissful all the time?" I asked while I poured some kibble into her bowl and topped it with a couple spoons of wet food. "Here you go, Princess Pinky."

I'd given her so many nicknames like Princess Pinky, the name I called her whenever she donned her fashionable hot-pink turtleneck sweater. She also answered to The White Wolf and Puppy Girl. When she got older, I called her Lumpy Galore because she'd developed so many lumps and bumps all over her body.

"Don't worry about those," Dr. Winters, my vet, told me. "They're not cancer. Even humans get a bit lumpy in their old age."

"Something to look forward to," I said.

"Better than the alternative." He winked at me.

If only I'd met him before he tied the knot.

I often wondered how Blondie knew her many names. Angel told me that dogs were programmed to respond to affection and kindness, kind of like humans. Besides, nicknames signified belonging, something I longed for.

Our daily routine gave me a sense of empowerment—like I could take on the day, no matter what. But that wasn't the only benefit of living with Blondie. She also gave me a sense of purpose. I learned from

Portrait of my beautiful pound mutt Blondie (photograph by Susanne Hayek).

experience the significance of that feeling, especially for me. Blondie turned out to be the key to me finding meaning in my crazy world.

Then, it struck me. I could take this new, positive attitude into the dating world and finally learn the fine art of dating. If a date turned into a nightmare, I could head home to this loving being. She'd make everything right again.

My strategy? To begin with, find a dog park near me. That was where Angel had said I'd meet someone. Second, I'd consider dating as a numbers game—say yes to anyone and everyone who asked me out. The more I dated, the better possibility I had of finding Mr. Right. As the saying went, *You have to kiss a lot of frogs to meet your Prince Charming.*

* * *

I found the Laurel Canyon Dog Park not far from Angel's house. Situated at the bottom of a clearing off Mulholland Drive, almost hidden from view in the Hollywood Hills, the park became a private oasis for me and my golden mutt.

It was known as the very first dog park in Los Angeles. Dogs and their humans had three acres of green grass to frolic and socialize off leash. For Blondie and me, the park quickly became a fenced-in, safe sanctuary, far from the busy Los Angeles streets. I belonged there and hoped Angel's prophecy would come true.

Once voted Flirtiest Flirt in high school, I started to worry I'd lost my talent forever until I found Blondie. She helped me get my flirt back. Turned out, flirting was a bit like riding a horse. When you fell off, you had to get back on and ride.

I went on a date with a personable, fast-talking guy I'd met at the park.

He appeared on the outside to have it all together. I watched our dogs play while he ran back to his car and grabbed a copy of Glamour *magazine. The magazine had nominated Mr. Fast Talker as one of the most eligible bachelors that year. He returned from the parking lot and showed me the full-page spread. There he stood in his tux, hands dripping with jewels, his badass Doberman by his side. The self-proclaimed*

Blondie and her buddy, a Greyhound named Elliott who was rescued from the racetrack. I dated his daddy (author's photograph).

Beverly Hills Cat Burglar had gotten the magazine nomination due to his interesting career choice.

"I turned my life around in prison," Cat Burglar told me. "Now, I work with the police and security companies."

To me, his life sounded so romantic, like Cary Grant in To Catch a Thief. *Tempting. But the thought of me introducing a recovered cat burglar to my church-going folks? I couldn't.*

I had a brief fling with a younger dude who looked more like a Greek god than a mere dog-loving mortal.

Ryan owned a rescue dog, a greyhound named Elliott. Ryan, besides being a year shy of drinking legally, and his dog broke too many of my personal treasures to count. Every time they came over, something ended up destroyed. Ryan accidentally broke my plates and cups, and Elliott chewed on the legs of my secondhand couch and kitchen table.

One day, I found the two of them playing tug-of-war with my childhood favorite Raggedy Ann doll.

"Hey," I yelled, "don't ruin that!"

Elliott shook the doll like a rabid dog.

"I've had her since I was a baby."

Blondie gets her 15 minutes of fame at her birthday party with special guest Elvez, the Mexican Elvis (author's photograph).

6. Love Quest

Ryan tried to get the stuffed toy away from his dog, but he pulled her legs so hard that they broke off.

"Sorry about that," Ryan said.

He apologized so many times that his words no longer had meaning. Next!

I didn't find love there, but still, I adored that park. Blondie and I traveled the canyon to the park almost every day after work. I even threw my golden dog a birthday party there when she turned eight years old. Elvez, the Mexican Elvis, performed "You Ain't Nothin' but a Pound Dog." Blondie got presents along with her fifteen minutes of fame because the local ABC affiliate covered her birthday in the news. All that fun, but I still felt something was missing in my life.

The fear of being single forever no longer clouded my every waking moment. Even so, the terror of being an old maid could still drag me to my knees, especially on my birthday, New Year's Eve, or the worst, Valentine's Day. The hardest? Hiding my tears at weddings, especially watching the happy couple leave for their two-week Hawaiian honeymoon. I hadn't taken a vacation in years.

I didn't allow myself to wallow. Time was ticking. If I wanted to become one of those happy couples, I had to act. Maybe I'd be more successful if I looked at my unfortunate situation through an optimistic lens.

Like Angel had said, "Enjoy the journey, not just the destination."

Time to put this good advice into action.

* * *

"We're heading to Barnes & Noble today." I leashed Blondie for what I hoped would be an enlightening adventure.

Yes, I brought Blondie with me to the bookstore; I didn't even question it. Blondie and I were a team now.

Bookstores were a popular hangout in the '80s, and that day was no exception. You couldn't buy books online. There was no Internet. In order to pick up the latest bestseller, you had to visit the local bookstore. While there, customers could relax and enjoy a cup of coffee.

Blondie and I maneuvered though the crowd, checking out the well-curated collection of books. We passed people sitting in comfy chairs, reading. Others walked the aisles, searching genres of books I hadn't even known existed. The customers all had one thing in common. Everyone stopped whatever they were doing to watch us pass.

One woman said, "I didn't know dogs were allowed in here."

"They are," I answered, as if I knew.

Blondie and I headed straight to the self-help section and found only a couple of dating books that might help me in my determination to get married.

"Hmm.... *Women Who Love Too Much: When You Keep Wishing and Hoping He'll Change*," I said to Blondie.

Her ears perked up when I said the title.

The book, published in 1985 and written by Robin Norwood, quickly became a *New York Times* bestseller.

"The cover asks if you are a woman who loves too much," I said to my four-legged accomplice. "Well, that's me."

Blondie sniffed the floor, dragged me, book in hand, to the end of the self-help aisle, and licked up a tiny sliver of a potato chip.

"Don't eat that!"

She swallowed.

"Listen, I need you to be serious here," I told Blondie. "This has to do with you too, girl. My future husband will become your daddy."

Blondie wagged her tail, excited about the prospect—or maybe she wagged it because she was reliving the taste of that crumb. I pulled her back to the self-help section, hoping for more encouragement.

I placed the book on the floor next to Blondie. She sniffed it in agreement.

I picked up *Codependent No More: How to Stop Controlling Others and Start Caring for Yourself*, written by Melody Beattie, who became a household name in recovery circles. The first edition was published in 1992 by Hazelden.

"Maybe I should read this one," I said to my blonde sidekick, now curled up in a ball on the cool tiled floor.

Too busy trying to fix my love life, I didn't notice that customers had to step over her to get by.

"The author says she had to battle codependence herself," I whispered to Blondie, "and writes that it *is* possible to crawl out of the abyss of pleasing others."

Blondie looked up at me as if I'd told her I found the cure for parvo.

The last phrase stuck a chord in me. "The abyss of pleasing others—perfectly stated. I'll tell you this, I'm not dating anyone who doesn't love my dog."

Blondie and I got more stares and whispers from customers on the way to check-out. I sort of liked the attention.

6. Love Quest

I didn't find any other books on the topic that sounded interesting to me back then. But still, I couldn't wait to dig into the two books that appeared to have a good handle on my people-pleasing issues.

*   *   *

Within a couple of days, I devoured both books, seeing my unhealthy relationship tendencies illuminated. Blondie didn't seem to care about my codependent behavior. She didn't take advantage of me either. Were there men like that?

"Now that I know what's wrong with me, how do I find Mr. Right? Is there a book for that?"

Blondie stared back at me.

"I feel like Dorothy in *The Wizard of Oz*," I said. "There's nothing for me behind that curtain, Mr. Wizard."

I realized there wasn't a magic wand that would bring me my Mr. Wonderful. But Dorothy hadn't had one either. She'd had the power to get herself home the entire time, thanks to her ruby red slippers. I didn't have any red slippers but felt confident I could find the solution to my problem on my own.

My love quest started at the beach. On an overcast summer evening, the full moon peeking from behind thick fog, Blondie and I howled at the moon to summon Mr. Right. We listened, but no one howled back. The Pacific Ocean was calm, serene, indifferent.

I stuffed a love letter I'd composed, sealed with a kiss, into a beautiful blue bottle, put in the cork, and threw it in the ocean. Blondie and I watched it bob and weave through the waves, only to land back on the sand at our feet.

"Blondie, looks like it's you and me."

Blondie barked in agreement.

I picked up the bottle, and we headed back to the car. "You're my true soulmate."

I lit candles at a Catholic church and asked God to send me a wonderful husband. Weeks went by. No one showed up.

I asked an Episcopal priest to pray for me, hoped that his connection to God might bring me what I wanted. Not. Maybe I had to become an Episcopalian before God would meddle in my business. Not a bad idea. My parents encouraged me to meet a man in church. That was how they'd met. Besides, Angel attended an Episcopalian church. I'd consider it a possible option. I figured a little spirituality couldn't hurt.

I'm Not Single, I Have a Dog

"Desperate times call for desperate measures," I told Blondie one morning while reading the newspaper. "Never thought I'd have to resort to taking out an ad."

Attracting men had never posed a problem before. My main issue was to find a way to stop following my heart and start listening to my head.

Mom had a solution. She'd told me I should randomly pick one of the many who asked me out and get married. I told her I didn't want to settle.

I wanted to feel loved and respected, find an equal who'd enrich my life, not destroy me. Maybe I'd find him in a newspaper ad.

My personal ad read:

> Love Me, Love My Dog.
> Twenty-something blonde seeks a serious relationship.
> I love my job, working as a publicist in Beverly Hills, and I'm passionate about finding the right man to balance my busy life. Could that be you?
> Must be in your mid- to late thirties with a good career path of your own. Must also be ready to fall in love with my pound mutt, Blondie.

A few hours after my ad came out, I received 197 phone messages in my newspaper mailbox.

"Blondie, your daddy's gotta be one of these callers! Let's listen."

I put my phone on speaker and hit the play button.

"Hello, I'm calling about your ad. I have a pot-bellied pig and a goat. I'm a real animal lover—"

Blondie listened intently with an adorable head tilt.

"Nope. We are not living on a farm."

"I live with my parents, and we have this dog we need to train to stop pissing in the house. I wanted to know if you could help—"

Blondie lay down, looking bored.

"No way. I'm looking for love, not a job potty-training your puppy."

"Hi. I have thirteen dogs and five cats, and I'm answering your ad—"

"Really? A hoarder?"

Blondie covered her face with her paws.

We spent a couple of hours fast-forwarding through all the pathetic messages until the machine came to this: "I like your ad. Do you like snakes? I have lots of snakes."

"Snakes? I hate snakes!"

I couldn't listen to any more. I felt overwhelmed with idiots. I punched the stop button.

6. Love Quest

"Blondie, why can't I meet a healthy man who has a job and likes dogs? Is that asking too much?"

She looked up at me and wagged her tail. Thank God for Blondie. Men could come and go. My faithful friend, Blondie, would stay.

7

The Law of Attraction

I decided to turn my attention inward. I still had my eyes open for Mr. Right. In fact, I'd become a dating machine. I'd read somewhere that a child's brain developed more from birth to age five than at any other time in life. The quality of a child's experiences in the first few years—whether positive or negative—lay the foundation as to how they'd perceive the world and these experiences were often reflected in their adult lives. That was it. My parents had fucked me up. Only I could fix me.

"I'm going to treat myself the way you treat me," I said to Blondie.

She wagged her feathered tail. When she saw me grab her leash, she broke out in her happy dance.

"We're headed to Angel's for what she calls an art-filled afternoon of self-discovery. Doesn't that sound exciting?"

Blondie obviously thought so. She pulled me out the door.

We arrived at Angel's, ready to get to work.

"Remember to keep your attention on your intentions," Angel said.

She led us upstairs to one of her extra bedrooms. Her entire home looked like a page from a Ralph Lauren Home catalog. It was no surprise, as Angel and the famous designer were good friends. The bedrooms were decorated with luxurious RL floral bedding and mismatched curtains, tied together with simple throw pillows.

"Even your house has style," I said. "Chic yet comfortable."

"Did you know this used to be a barn?"

"What?" I asked. "Are you kidding?"

"It was a complete mess, but I saw real potential." She gestured toward a long hallway. "The bedrooms were once horse stalls, and the upstairs used to be the hayloft."

She opened a door to her craft room. In true Angel style, she had prepared a table for today's project with everything we needed for our vision boards—poster boards, magazines, newspapers, pens, crayons, paper, notecards, sticky notes, and glue.

"Let's have some fun," she said with a grin. "Keep in mind, creating a vision board is all about self-discovery and manifestation."

We sat across from each other, and I thought about the times we'd spent in this room over the years, working on various projects.

In December, we called Angel's craft room Santa Central, the place dedicated to wrapping Christmas presents. It took Angel the entire month and help from friends like me to prepare for Santa's arrival. Even after the girls had grown up, Angel continued with the tradition.

"We both know what I want," I said. "But how about you? What do you want to manifest?"

"Abundance," she answered. "Abundance of love, peace, and happiness for my family and friends."

Have yourself a merry little Christmas...
love, Blondie and Susan

A Christmas card from me and Blondie (photograph by Susanne Hayek).

I should have known Angel's vision board would be about manifesting for everyone in her life; she always thought about others, but not in a codependent way.

I opened an issue of *Vogue* and scanned the pages, looking for something that represented my future. I relished our craft nights. But that evening, I couldn't wait to share my exciting news.

"Well, your wish has already manifested for me," I said, my smile as big as the iconic Hollywood sign. "I met not one, but two guys."

"See? I told you Blondie would lead you to your future husband." Her sky-blue eyes sparkled with wonder.

Angel never wore make-up—ever. Her natural beauty was accentuated by her perfect profile, high cheekbones, and nose that turned up ever so slightly.

"Blondie had nothing to do with it," I said. "I met James at a charity art auction."

"A charity art auction," Angel said. "How fancy."

I found an ad featuring an athletic-looking young woman tying her shoes to prepare for a run. The pretty blonde had a dog with pointy ears by her side, who reminded me of Blondie. In the distance, a hunk of a man could be seen running toward her.

"This is a picture to aspire to," I said, showing the image to Angel.

She nodded, and I placed the image in my growing pile.

"I wonder if James runs. He goes to USC, studying to be a doctor."

"Ooh, a doctor in the family. I like him already!"

Angel gave me a high five when she found the word *abundance* in a magazine. "See? Abundance is already happening all around me."

"Blondie might not have been with you when you met James, but I've noticed your positive attitude since you brought her home. That attitude attracts people to you." Angel handed me an image she'd cut out of a young couple embracing. "This one's for you."

The woman in the photo had blonde hair like mine. She gazed intensely into her partner's eyes. Behind them stood a single-story house, complete with a white picket fence—an ideal family home. It looked a little too perfect to be real, but I pasted it to my board.

"The guy in this photo kind of reminds me of Bobby, the musician I met." My stomach flip-flopped at the mention of his name.

"Another musician?" She shook her head. "You've been down that road before."

"This one actually makes a living from writing songs," I said. "The night I met him, he had the whole bar singing one of his hits."

"As long as he makes a living, I guess—"

"You know I have a soft spot for musicians," I cut in.

"Me too." Angel put her scissors down and leaned back in her chair. "I fell for a rock star before I met John."

"You never told me about that."

I found an image of a family at the beach. The mother was applying sunscreen to her daughter, and the father was holding his son's hand as they walked together toward the waves. A keeper for sure.

Angel continued, "He bought us a pair of parakeets ... so romantic. We named them Ike and Tina Turner," her chin quivered. "He turned out to be the Ike type. I kept the birds but ditched the guy."

"He hit you?"

"No, darling, but he threatened to," Angel sighed. "Made me feel unworthy. Turned my entire world into a chaotic mess."

"I didn't know. I assumed you'd lived such a charmed life."

"I do now. But there are some skeletons in my closet," she said. "It took a while, but I finally got up the courage to break it off."

"I need courage like that," I muttered. "I have a hard time letting anyone go, especially asshole men."

"It's never easy, but every woman must learn to protect herself." Angel reached across the table and took my hand in hers. "Promise me you'll never put up with abuse, physical or mental."

"I promise."

But her words triggered something. I stuffed the feeling down and went back to my vision board.

"Creating a vision board is a little like planting a seed," she said. "This process helps plant your intentions."

"My intentions are clear," I said.

I pasted magazine letters to the top of my vision board, spelling the words *Happily Ever After*.

Angel saw the words. "That's brilliant," she said. "No more obsessing. You've put your intention into the world. Sit back and watch everything you've dreamed about become reality."

She picked up a red marker and drew a giant heart around the image pasted on her board. To illustrate abundance, Angel chose an expanse of ocean, an eagle flying high against the vast blue sky, and a forest of giant redwood trees with the sun shining through in streaks. She held up her masterpiece.

"You could sell that," I said.

"And you could be married to a doctor or a rich musician by this time next year." Angel giggled.

You never know... I crossed myself. "I have dates with both of them this weekend."

"I'm so proud of you," Angel said. "First dates can be as stressful as job interviews. Just don't jump into a relationship. Take your time."

"And then there's the question of what to do at the end of a date," I said. "That's the part I find painfully awkward. Do I give a big hug? How about a kiss? What if I don't want to kiss him?"

"Don't get ahead of yourself," Angel said. "Listen to your gut. Any time I feel my gut recoil, there's a logical reason. Sometimes, it takes a while for me to understand what it's telling me. But your gut is always right."

"What if my gut doesn't tell me anything?" I pasted the last image on my board. A beautiful nineteenth-century church, the perfect place for an intimate wedding ceremony.

"It took me years of therapy to learn to trust mine," she said. "Maybe make an appointment with my shrink."

"Maybe, but I don't make enough money right now."

"She'll see you on a sliding scale," Angel said.

"I'm sure I could use some guidance." I shrugged. "Couldn't everyone? I'll think about it."

"I'll give you her number before you leave."

I nodded, but I knew I wasn't going to make that call anytime soon.

"But what about this weekend? What if I choose the wrong guy?"

"Just don't rush into anything," Angel said. "Notice the twinges your gut sends you."

With both our vision boards ready to make a difference in our lives, it was now time to clean up. I helped Angel stack the magazines and throw away any paper scraps left behind. That was when I noticed the quote she'd added in her perfect cursive handwriting, accenting every capital letter with curlicues.

"*Abundance is a process of letting go*," I read. "*That which is empty can receive*." I looked at her. "I love this, but how do I let go of my past shitty relationships?"

"Work by emptying the self-critical tapes that play in your head," she said. "That is crucial. Both our mothers were not the best at nurturing. Neither did much for our emotional development. It's up to us to learn and grow."

"You can say that again," I agreed.

8

Barking Up the Wrong Tree

"All these clothes and nothing to wear," I said to Blondie.

She watched me take shirts, pants, and even dresses out of my closet, only to throw them in a heap on my bed.

"I've got to have something to wear on my date with James. He's taking me to the Greek Theatre."

Blondie jumped and twirled like she wanted to come to the concert too.

"Sorry, sweet baby girl, no doggies allowed."

I tried on everything and finally settled on my favorite pair of black jeans and my new black V-neck blouse with the puffy sleeves. The final touch, my sexy, strappy sandals. Black, still my go-to color.

All dressed up, and I felt like a total loser. I wondered what preppy James would think about me. He reminded me of a poodle, perfectly groomed with his shiny, manicured fingernails.

"Why am I going through all this, Blondie?" I felt like an ugly mutt. "We both know he'll never fall for someone like me."

Even Blondie's amber eyes couldn't make my anxiety go away.

When I looked at myself in the mirror, Dad's words echoed in my head.

"You're a Hartzler. We're perfect."

When Dad said I had to be perfect, he meant it. Impossible for their youngest—me. My teenage self knew I'd never be perfect, but if Daddy wanted perfection, I'd sure try.

Blondie didn't expect me to be anything but myself. Maybe James would too.

I stroked Blondie's back, relaxed a bit ... and then—*uh-oh*—my doorbell rang. Blondie jumped off the couch and barked in alert.

Blondie went crazy.

"I know; someone's at the door." I opened the door, and she lunged at the stranger standing on my porch.

"You didn't tell me you had a killer dog," James said, his hands in the air.

"Blondie, it's okay, baby," I said. "This is James, a friend."

Blondie relented and rolled over in submission.

"Come in," I said to James.

"No, no," James said, stepping backward. "We've got to get going. Might hit some traffic."

He wore his brown hair short and groomed to perfection. He made me want to mess it up. I resisted; I had to make a good first impression like he did in his gray suit with crisp white button-down shirt.

Calm now, Blondie looked up at James, but he didn't acknowledge her. I gave her a kiss and a rub on the top of her head and then closed the door behind me.

"Sorry about Blondie," I said. "I've never seen her like that."

"I'm so psyched about tonight," James said, completely ignoring my comment about my dog.

Maybe her barking annoyed him.

I couldn't help but notice his walk while on the way to his car. Rather than taking steps, James took long strides, as if he was in a real hurry.

"You look nice." A true gentleman, he grabbed my hand and led me to the passenger door of a jet-black Porsche 911.

At least my outfit matched his car. Good first step, we both liked the color black.

James opened the passenger door. "My lady." He motioned for me to take a seat.

"Fancy ride." I didn't feel good enough to be with a man like James, one who drove a luxury sports car. I crumpled into the passenger seat like the heap of clothes I'd left on my bed.

"My parents bought it for me when I graduated college."

The engine purred, and my heart raced with anxiety.

"Nice parents. Mine gave me a lamp when I graduated." My cheeks burned. *Why did I admit that?*

"A lamp? That's weird."

Oh no, he thinks I'm weird. Quick, say something funny.

"So are my parents. I've never understood why everyone likes them so much," I said. "Friends from high school still visit them."

That wasn't funny. I wanted to kick myself.

"They can't be that bad. They raised *you.*"

I heard what he'd said, but I couldn't find the words to respond.

8. Barking Up the Wrong Tree

Maybe he likes me. Keep your cool, girl.

"What kind of doctor are you studying to be?"

"Pediatric oncologist."

What a catch!

"That's noble of you," I said in a low, steady voice even though I wanted to scream and jump for joy.

"Not really. Came naturally to me. I had a cousin who died after battling cancer when we were young. I decided that when I grew up, I'd save kids like her."

A doctor who helps kids. I couldn't believe my luck.

"Unless you count Siesta, my childhood dog, I've never had anyone close to me die. Don't know what I'd do."

"I hadn't, either. It scared me so much as a kid. I didn't want anyone else in my family to have to go through that pain again. So my goal is to put an end to cancer someday."

"I can't even imagine."

But I could imagine James, naked, in my bed.

"How about you?" James asked. "Did you always want to be in public relations?"

"Not really," I said. "I majored in journalism. Became the first female sportswriter for my college newspaper. I wanted to get inside men's locker rooms."

"That's funny." He turned to look at me. I noticed his long eyelashes that framed his deep brown eyes. I could get lost in those eyes. "So were men's locker rooms all you'd dreamed of?"

"I never got to find out. Ended up writing about women's sports."

James pulled into the parking lot and headed straight to the valet. Now, this guy knew how to live. Me, on the other hand, I sounded so ridiculous with my weird parents and my desire to see naked men in locker rooms. Here was this great guy, and I was coming off as a complete idiot.

I took a deep breath when we got to our seats—front and center, some of the best seats in the house. I tried my best to act normal. The grandeur of the Griffith Park trees that surrounded the Greek Theatre took the edge off. Nature always had a way of steadying me.

Even as a child, when things had gone haywire in my family, our half-acre backyard had become my own private Eden, where I felt safe with Siesta always by my side. That dog ... I'd felt more attached to Siesta than to the humans in my family.

From the outside, we looked like the perfect family, but inside, Mom raged, and Dad stayed away from the drama by hiding at the office. Erin, Will, and I never knew what would set Mom off.

Don't get me wrong; there was never any physical abuse. Mom never hit us, but she did hit at us with a fly swatter. She'd line the three of us up on the couch and threaten us with that fly swatter like a lion tamer. Having three kids in four years with an absent husband must have overwhelmed her.

As a child, I blamed myself for all the chaos in my family. I learned how to pretend to be perfect to stay out of trouble. As an adult, I dated losers to feel good about myself in comparison.

James looked at me with his bright eyes and said, "Want a beer?"

"Oh, sure, thanks!" Maybe a beer would calm me down.

When James left me in my seat, I felt relieved to have a few moments alone. *I closed my eyes and realized I'd rather be at home with my dog than at the concert with this man. Maybe the soft night air would to do its magic.*

Everything's fine, I repeated to myself over and over.

When James returned and handed me a beer, I held out a twenty-dollar bill.

"What's that for?" James asked. "You don't owe me anything. This is a date, remember? And the guy pays."

"But you're a student," I said.

"My parents help me out financially. They expect me to have fun once in a while."

What a novel idea—parents who wanted their kids to have fun. Made me think of another piece of Dad's wisdom he'd bestowed upon me back when I was in the fifth grade.

"Life's not all fun and games," Dad said.

He knew I liked to socialize more than study.

"Why not?" I replied.

"Because it's not; that's why."

I had known I'd make Dad angry when he saw my most recent report card, but what could I do? I'd had to show it to him. At eight, I didn't get straight As like Erin and Will.

Later, I'd learn Erin and Will hadn't gotten excellent grades either, but back then, I'd believed my sister and brother were way smarter than me. I wondered why Dad's words still tortured me.

At twilight, the show started. Concertgoers jumped to their feet and danced to the Eurythmics. Annie Lennox belted out my favorite song, "Would I Lie to You?" James sprang up from his seat, grabbed my hand, and pulled me up with him. He twirled me right there in the aisle. I started to move to the music but felt awkward and self-conscious.

All of a sudden, I thought about Bobby, the musician I'd met. When the song ended, I lied to James and told him I needed to hit the ladies' room.

I pulled the slip of paper with Bobby's phone number out of my purse. At the phone booth, I froze with indecision until a woman bumped into me. That was when I dialed Bobby's number out of my purse. His answering machine picked up.

"Lynn and I aren't home right now. Leave a message."

Did I dial the right number? I didn't recognize Bobby's voice on the machine. *And who's Lynn?*

9

Rolling Over

The date ended without incident and I found James impossibly handsome. Still, couldn't stop thinking about Bobby.

What the hell's up with his answering machine? I called him first thing the next morning to find out. If Bobby had lied to me, then forget him. I'd concentrate my energies on James.

"Are you married or something?" I needed the truth, deciding to broach the topic head-on.

"No, ma'am," Bobby said in a singsong voice. "Why do you ask?"

"There's a strange man on your answering machine." I bit my lower lip.

"Oh, um, must've given you the wrong number."

"I dialed the same number as last night and you just answered. You sure you don't have a girlfriend or a wife you're hiding?" I joked. *But who forgets their phone number?*

"I'm hoping you'll be my girlfriend," he said, changing the subject.

His words gave me goose bumps. *Could Bobby be the one?*

"Well, maybe that can be arranged." I twirled my hair.

I wanted to believe Bobby, so of course I did, ignoring the red flag that waved in my face.

Bobby asked, "Want me to come over?"

"Now? It's only eleven in the morning. I thought we'd planned to get together for dinner."

"We did, but hearing your voice makes me want to see you right away."

I couldn't wait to see him either.

"Can't stop thinking about you, babe."

While I was flattered that Bobby wanted to rush over, that meant I had to get myself and my place ready and fast.

"Well, I guess so. Give me an hour."

* * *

9. Rolling Over

Luckily, I'd vacuumed and dusted my living room the night before for my big date with James. At least the living room looked decent. Now to make the bedroom presentable. In my tiny place, he'd have to walk though that room if he needed to use the bathroom. And the kitchen too. A total disaster area. *What if he wanted to get himself a glass of water or something?*

I got to work, hid my dirty dishes in the stove, stuffed the clothes I'd left strewed all over my bedroom in the closet, and shoved a bunch of stuff under the bed. A few minutes left to get ready. The hot rollers came out of my hair the moment the doorbell rang.

Blondie yowled like a wild coyote.

"Welcome to the doghouse," I yelled at the door over her loud barks.

Instead of coming inside, Bobby got down on his knees and motioned for Blondie to come. She stopped the ruckus, wagged her tail, trotted over to him, and gave him a big, wet, sloppy kiss.

"I think she likes you," I said.

"I'm good with animals," Bobby said and looked up at me with his puppy-dog eyes.

To me, Bobby's tenderness with Blondie meant I could trust him. If Blondie liked him, I liked him. James hadn't crooned over her like that. He'd barely noticed her.

Bobby grabbed a small box he had hidden behind him and placed it on my coffee table.

A present for me? Already? I glanced inside. Saw a toothbrush. *Maybe he's a stickler for keeping his teeth clean?*

"Planning to move in?" I pointed at his box.

"No, I brought you something." He pulled out a bottle of wine and handed it to me. "Here."

"Red. My fave. We'll open this later."

I duped myself into believing his box held stuff he needed for the day, like the nice bottle of wine he'd brought for me.

"Here, have a seat." I motioned for him to sit on my couch. "Can I get you anything?"

"Just you."

I sat down at the other end of the couch, and Bobby slid his way next to me. He smelled like Good & Plenty candies. When he looked deep into my eyes, I realized the hunky musician's eyes were the same color as Blondie's—amber.

"Your eyes are stunning," I said.

"Yeah, if you like shit brown," Bobby said with a devilish grin.

"Don't say that. Look, they're the same amber color as Blondie's."

At the sound of her name, Blondie turned and looked at us.

"No way, babe. Blondie's are way prettier than mine."

"You both have these tiny gold specs," I said.

We were so close that I could feel his moist breath on my face. Bobby put his arm around me and tenderly pulled me into him. We kissed slow, luscious kisses with warm, tight hugs. I relaxed into him. Bobby made me feel desirable.

"You're so beautiful," Bobby said.

How I'd always craved to hear those words. I closed my eyes, ready for more when Bobby stood up. He gently took my hand in his to pull me into my bedroom.

"I don't think that's a good idea," I said.

"Shh, love's always a good idea."

I couldn't argue with love; that was all I'd ever wanted.

"Wait," I said. "Do you have a condom?"

Bobby pulled a Trojan out of his wallet.

"Go make yourself comfortable. I have to get myself ready too."

In the bathroom, I added my own birth control—my diaphragm, a contraceptive sponge, and lots of spermicide. I didn't need to go so overboard with my birth control. I took the pill.

My extreme caution had stemmed from my first serious relationship. Larry, my college sweetheart, the guy I had given my virginity to at twenty, knocked me up. I'd met the native New Yorker at *The Daily Aztec* where I'd gotten my first writing job at San Diego State University.

The summer before my senior year, I visited him and his family in Queens. His parents insisted we sleep in separate rooms, but that didn't keep us apart. One night, Larry took me to the Kosciuszko Bridge, which connected Queens and Brooklyn. Right there in the backseat of his parents' Buick, we made love. Of course, I hadn't thought about protection. Larry had convinced me we would be safe as long as he pulled out before ejaculation. I guessed, that night, with the moon waxing and the stars shining, he forgot. And I ended up pregnant.

I went to my college health center.

"I can't be pregnant," I told the nurse, crying hysterically. "My mom will kill me if she finds out."

The nurse remained professional, as if scheduling an abortion happened every day at SDSU. "She doesn't have to know if you have an abortion."

9. Rolling Over

I never told Mom. Years later, I still burst into tears when I think about the baby that could have been.

"Get over here," Bobby said. "I want you so bad."

*   *   *

I stayed in bed with Bobby all through the night and most of that Sunday. Bobby in my bed felt right, which should've been another red flag. I didn't know him. But Bobby looked good, he knew how to please me in bed, and he loved Blondie. What more did I need?

That night, I spooned Blondie, and Bobby spooned both of us until my alarm went off.

"Oh shit. Monday morning," I said. "Got to get my ass to work."

Bobby groaned and rolled over in my bed. I groped for my clothes in the dark and got ready for work in the bathroom.

"Sorry to wake you, Mr. Sleeping Beauty. Would you mind walking Blondie for me this morning? I'm running late. Her leash is hanging by the front door. Thanks!"

I felt so pleased to have someone I trusted to walk Blondie for me.

All day at work, I fantasized about a future with Bobby, certain I'd met my soulmate. We'd get married and have a couple kids. I hoped I could believe our perfect future into reality.

I couldn't wait to get home after a long day. Maybe Bobby would call. Or even come over again.

Blondie greeted me with her happy dance.

"You smell so good, girlie girl." I bent down to give her a kiss.

"I gave her a bath." Bobby stomped into my living room like he lived there, a beer in his hand.

"You're still here?"

I didn't mind. In fact, I felt euphoric that Bobby wanted to stay with me. My last heartbreak never stuck around.

"I cleaned your entire place," he announced with his arms out wide.

I looked around. Everything was spotless.

"And rearranged your closet." He pointed to my bedroom. "A total mess."

"You did all that for me?"

It didn't occur to me to be concerned. Instead, I saw Bobby's poking around my stuff as proof that he cared about me. The idea of him organizing my life while I worked gave me what I called my Stevie Motner feeling.

In grade school, my classmate Stevie Motner had taken care of me.

He followed me around to make sure my shoes were tied and that I'd remembered my lunch. I hadn't felt that cherished since the sixth grade.

"Wow, thanks so much."

"No problem. Made dinner too. Here, sit down."

At the kitchen table, Bobby pulled out my chair like a gentleman and set a simple pasta dish in front of me. He'd used the fresh tomatoes I'd bought that weekend. He poured me the final glass of red wine left from the bottle he had given me the night before.

"Delicious," I said. "I could get used to this."

Bobby grabbed a plate for himself and opened himself another beer. He sat down next to me. "At your service."

I noticed the dishes I'd hidden Sunday night now sparkled in the drying rack. "Did you do my dishes too?"

"Yes, ma'am. Can't stand dirty dishes. Found where you hid them in the oven. What do you say if we put a new coat of paint in here, babe?"

"You paint too?"

"I'm a man of many talents." He winked at me.

"I'm sure you have better things to do, like writing hit songs."

"I'm a musician, true, but I haven't made it yet."

"But you told me you wrote the song 'Jump.' You must have made a fortune from that."

"I thought you knew; I joked about writing that song. Van Halen writes their own songs."

"I'm so gullible. But how can you afford to live in that swanky apartment building?"

"That apartment's not mine, babe. I've been housesitting for friends." He twirled some pasta onto his fork.

"So where do you live?"

"In Mandeville Canyon."

At least he lives in an upscale neighborhood, I thought.

I didn't find out until much later that he lived in an old, run-down trailer parked on a friend's property.

"That's a long drive from here."

"Tell me about it." He slurped up a piece of pasta. "I don't have my own wheels right now. Got in a bad accident a few months ago and totaled my car."

"How can you live in LA without a car?"

"Sure, it's not easy, but I make it work. I'll have to leave soon to catch the late bus."

I hesitated. This guy wasn't the successful musician he'd said he was, he didn't live around the corner like I'd thought, and he didn't even have a car. But something about Bobby drew me to him. He seemed so kind and was a true romantic. Look at all the things he had done for me. Maybe he was a little rough around the edges, but he had so much potential. And he loves my dog.

"Well, I guess you could stay here for a while, so you can paint my apartment."

I couldn't decide if allowing him to stay with me so soon was a good idea or not, but I couldn't say no to someone so handsome and nice. Besides, Blondie seemed to approve. That was good enough for me.

10

The Fur Flies

Bobby and I had been dating ... er, living together ... for a few weeks. Embarrassed about moving him in with me too quickly, I kept our living arrangement secret from everyone, even Angel.

I liked living with Bobby. In the beginning, it was glorious. We never argued. He kept my apartment spotless and even did my laundry without asking. Bobby made me coffee every morning before I left for work and looked after Blondie while I was gone all day. When we ate at home, he always cooked and even made me romantic candlelit dinners from time to time. Besides, it was a relief to finally have a plus-one for all the Hollywood soirees I got invited to due to my work as a publicist.

Bobby didn't judge me; he accepted me unconditionally, just like Blondie. I thought that was enough. But looking back, I can't help but think, who was I kidding?

I remembered the morning after our first bender together.

"I've never felt so comfortable with anyone," I told him. "Who else would hold my hair back while I barfed in the toilet all night?"

"I tried to stop you," Bobby said, "but you just had to have that last martini."

"Don't remind me. Guess I lost count."

Turned out, I was flawed—still am—like everyone else in the world. I wasn't perfect like Dad wanted. Bobby didn't care much about my foibles.

Bobby hid little love notes for me around the house. I'd open a drawer to find a sticky note with a big red heart. Another one of his sweet notes I found hidden under my pillow, and it reminded me of how much he loved me. I found them in cupboards, drawers, and even pasted to my television set. Those little love notes captured my heart and hooked me. I finally felt ready to bring Bobby out of the shadows.

"I can't wait for you to meet Bobby," I told Angel over the phone, twirling my hair.

"About time I get to meet this mysterious man of yours," Angel said.

10. The Fur Flies

I felt a flutter in my belly.

"I'm envisioning hosting your wedding in my backyard."

"Now, who's getting ahead of herself?" I asked with a snicker.

"I'm just so excited for you."

"Me too. But I need you to give me your honest opinion."

"Of course, darling," Angel agreed. "Why don't you bring him over for dinner tonight? That way, the whole family can meet him."

Bobby, Blondie, and I jumped in my car later that evening and headed to Angel's home. I bit my nails on the way, worried that Bobby wouldn't make a good first impression.

"Be on your best behavior," I said. "She's one of my dearest friends."

"Promise," Bobby said, smelling the flowers I'd bought for him to give Angel—her favorite, yellow roses.

I liked them too, especially after learning that yellow roses stood for friendship.

I tucked a piece of his hair behind his ear at the front door. When Angel opened it, her three dogs sprinted to greet Blondie. They didn't even notice the stranger, Bobby, in their presence.

"Angel, this is Bobby," I said.

Bobby bowed his head as if he were meeting the Queen of England. He handed her the bouquet.

"Thank you, Bobby," Angel said, hugging him. "Susan has told me all about you. Come in."

I caught a whiff of her famous chicken wings in the oven when I stepped inside. Bobby and I followed Angel into the kitchen.

"Can I get you anything to drink?" Angel asked.

"I'll have a beer," Bobby answered before I could get a word out. "If you have any."

"Of course we do." Angel, the hostess with the mostest, opened her fully-stocked refrigerator.

"I'm driving," I said, "so water for me."

"A simple dinner is on the menu tonight," Angel said. "Chicken wings and a nice crisp salad. If you'd like, Bobby, I can make you some pasta too. That's all the girls will eat these days."

"Smells good, whatever's in there," Bobby said, pointing to the oven.

That was when I noticed Blondie had broken from her pack to hover in the kitchen. She couldn't stay away from the aroma of Angel's wings roasting.

"You sneaky little thing you," I said to Blondie. "One whiff of poultry, and nothing else in the world matters."

"We're back," John said.

John and the girls, eight-year-old Percy and eleven-year-old Presley, walked into the kitchen, wearing matching baseball caps.

"Darling." Angel kissed each of them. "This is Bobby, Susan's new boyfriend."

Hearing her introduce him as my boyfriend gave me goose bumps.

"A pleasure," John said and shook Bobby's hand.

"Why don't you boys get to know each other in the dining room?" Angel said. "Dinner's almost ready. Girls, go get cleaned up."

"Angel, let me help you," I said. A few minutes alone would give me a chance to hear what she thought about my new beau.

"He's so handsome," Angel whispered. Her face beamed. "And he seems really nice."

My heart swelled. Angel liked Bobby. My life could finally begin.

From the kitchen, I overheard John and Bobby yakking it up, only to be interrupted by two noisy kids, Percy and Presley, running in to take their seats.

"I coach the girls' softball team," I heard John tell Bobby.

"We won again, Mom," Percy yelled.

"I knew you would," Angel said.

I followed her to the dining room. Angel carried a tray of chicken wings. I brought the salad and a warmed fresh baguette to the table.

"They made the finals," John said, his chin high.

"That's great," Bobby said. "Do you mind if I have another?" He pointed to his now-empty beer.

"Of course not," Angel said. "Help yourself."

Bobby headed back to the kitchen to do just that—help himself. I noticed a serious look on his face when he returned to the table.

Oh no, something's wrong. I knew Bobby was too good to be true.

I braced myself for the worst.

"I'd like to say a little grace before we eat"—Bobby pulled his chair to the table—"if that's okay."

You could've picked my mouth up off the floor. I looked from Bobby to Angel, hoping his idea would be welcome.

"Not only is that okay"—Angel nodded—"it's also utterly divine."

Bobby nodded solemnly, reached over, took my hand in his, and closed his eyes.

"Thank you, Father, for bringing Susan into my life," Bobby prayed. "And thank you, Angel, for preparing this wonderful meal. Amen."

"I didn't know you prayed," I said.

"Doesn't everyone?" Bobby answered, turning on that devilish grin again.

"I, for one, believe in the power of prayer," Angel said. She closed her eyes and added, "Thank you, God, for my family and friends."

"I concur," John said. "Let's eat."

"You guys make a funny couple," Presley said, twirling her pasta on a fork.

"Funny? How?" I asked.

"You're, like, a secretary," Presley said, her mouth full. "He's, like, this cool rock-and-roll dude."

"Sweetheart"—Angel pressed her lips—"that's not very nice. And what have I told you about speaking with your mouth full?"

"Hey, what's that behind your ear?" Bobby scooted his chair near Presley.

She looked over her shoulder. "Nothin."

"I see something in there." Bobby moved closer. He put his hand next to her ear, and *voilà*, a quarter appeared.

"How'd you do that?" Presley giggled and grabbed the coin.

"It's magic," Bobby answered, fanning his hands in front of his face.

"Do it to me." Percy turned so that her ear faced Bobby.

Sure enough, he pulled a coin out of her ear too.

She shot Presley a look. "Can you cut my sister in half?"

"Children, let the man eat," John said. "So, Bobby, I can see you're talented. What do you do for a living?"

"I'm a musician, still struggling," Bobby said. "Have to keep my day job, painting houses. Just finished a job in Mandeville Canyon."

I almost snorted out loud. To my knowledge, Bobby hadn't worked a day since he moved in with me.

"We need our house painted," Angel said. "You'll have to give us an estimate."

"Happy to," Bobby said and stood up to get himself another beer.

Percy and Presley squirmed in their chairs; adult conversation bored them.

John to the rescue. "Girls, why don't you go watch some TV? I think *Family Ties* is starting soon."

When the meal was finished, Bobby surprised me again by helping with clean-up. I should have predicted he would with his obsession with cleaning. *What a great guy I'd found.*

On the way to the car, I said, "I didn't know you were a magician."

"I'm not." Bobby chuckled. "That's the only magic trick I know. Hey, I need you to make a quick stop. Got to pick up a six-pack."

"Didn't you drink enough already?" I remembered seeing a few empty bottles in my living room before we left, and I figured he'd drunk those earlier.

"Now you're monitoring how much I drink?" Bobby pulled Blondie in his lap, so she could stick her head out the window.

Blondie usually liked to let her fur fly in the wind but not that night. She struggled to get away from him.

"What are you doing?" I heard the edge in my voice.

Bobby kept a firm grip on her, forcing Blondie to stay on his lap.

She yelped. Her cry caused my mama bear to come out.

"Put her in the backseat *now*. You're drunk."

"Susan!"

My car swerved into oncoming traffic. Bobby prevented a head-on collision.

"Shit," Bobby said. He helped Blondie to the backseat. "I'm not an alcoholic, if that's what you're thinking."

"I'm sorry," I said, my voice cracking. "I didn't mean to accuse you of anything."

"You're one to talk, barfing all night after that party," Bobby reminded me.

I felt my chest tighten at the mere mention of that night.

I stopped to get another six-pack for him, even gave him the money to pay for it. He came back to the car with his favorite—Heineken.

Still, I wondered if Bobby did have a drinking problem. He drank beer every day, but so what? At least he didn't touch the strong stuff. I could help him stop.

Even if he did drink too much, what could I do about it? I wouldn't break up with him. Living alone seemed worse to me than putting up with Bobby's issues. Besides, he needed me, and I believed that was enough.

11

Lady and the Tramp

My apartment looked better than ever, thanks to Bobby adding a new coat of paint along with his diligence in keeping my tiny place spotless. He acted more like a wife than my boyfriend, and he seemed quite content with his role as a stay-at-home dog dad.

To show my appreciation, I paid for everything, even buying him new clothes when he needed them. I felt safe and thought Bobby would never leave me as long as I took care of his every need.

I wanted my love story with Bobby to be the image of a healthy, equal partnership and demonstrated my desire by treating Bobby the way I hoped he'd treat me. You know, the golden rule. I loved to make Bobby happy; his pleasure gave me a warm and fuzzy feeling inside.

By Thanksgiving, seven months after Bobby had moved in, I decided the time had come to introduce him to Mom and Dad. Erin wouldn't be celebrating with us. She spent most holidays with her husband and kids in Northern California. My brother, Will, lived in Oregon. He moved there for an MBA program, compliments of Mom and Dad, so he'd be a no-show too. It'd only be Bobby, Mom, Dad, Blondie, Terry the cat and me.

Bobby sat in the passenger seat on our way to the Valley. He stayed unusually quiet, gazing out the window.

"I figured out who you remind me of." I broke the silence. "Tramp from *Lady and the Tramp.* I love that movie. Forget about Prince Charming. Tramp did it for me."

"Thought you were going to say Don Johnson, but I'll take Tramp." Bobby put his head back and howled like a dog. "He's his own man—uh, dog."

I laughed out loud, but Bobby's howl made Blondie sit up in the backseat at attention.

"You're okay, girl," I said.

"She's not just okay," Bobby said. "She's the best dog in the world. Isn't that right, Blondie?"

"I couldn't agree more," I said. "Not to change the subject, Mr. Alpha Dog, but remember, Mom and Dad don't drink. Mom doesn't like it when I drink either, so don't expect any alcohol at the table."

"*A-roo*," Bobby howled again. "I know; you've warned me, babe. I've got it covered."

"They're pretty strict. Mom jokes that I can't drink until I'm fifty. And even then, only a sip at celebrations."

Bobby's eyes narrowed, and he patted the bag he held tenderly on his lap. "That's why I brought my own six-pack."

"I want you to make a good impression, that's all."

"I said, I know," Bobby said. "Quit ragging on me." He ripped open the bag, pulled out a beer, and downed it.

"Stop it! I could get cited for an open container."

Bobby opened a second beer and downed it too.

"What's wrong with you?" I asked. "Yesterday, you were so nice."

"You be nice to me, babe, and I'll be nice to you."

"I hate it when you get like this." I grabbed the steering wheel so tight that my knuckles turned white.

"Did you ever think that maybe I feel a little pressure about meeting your parents?" Bobby asked. "Mine weren't around much when I grew up."

"I know all about your lousy childhood," I said. "Don't bring that shitty attitude to Thanksgiving dinner. You're supposed to be grateful today."

"Grateful that I haven't seen my dad in five years? I don't even know where he is."

I didn't mean to hurt Bobby's feelings. I had my own anxiety about introducing him—or any man—to my parents. But his childhood seemed so tragic. I couldn't imagine not knowing where to find Mom and Dad. They'd lived in the same house since I was five.

"You're right," I said. "I should've thought about your feelings. I'm sorry about your dad."

"Last time I saw him, he'd hired my band to play at his sixth wedding," Bobby said. "Dad got shit-faced drunk with me and the boys. Don't know if he's still with that wife."

When we pulled into the driveway, I took a deep breath.

"You've got to leave those in the car." I pointed to his remaining beers. "Come on, we're late."

Bobby grimaced but complied with my request.

Phew! Awkward situation avoided.

11. Lady and the Tramp

When I opened the back gate, the truth hit me; Bobby did have a drinking problem.

* * *

"This turkey is excellent, Mrs. Hartzler," Bobby said.

Mom didn't answer; she barely looked at my beau. The dining room was so quiet that you could hear Mom's fancy silverware scrape against her good china.

"Suzie tells us you're a musician," Dad said.

"That's right, sir." Bobby shoveled more food into his mouth.

"I'm a musician too," Dad said proudly. "I play the trumpet and sing. My band is called The Sometimers. Guess why."

"I have no idea," Bobby said, his mouth full.

"Because, sometimes, we're good," Dad said with a grin, "and, sometimes, we're bad."

"That's funny." Bobby nodded, forcing a smile.

I prayed Dad wouldn't add the fact that, as a kid, I sang "Hello, Dolly" with The Sometimers. *Such a geek.*

"I also paint houses," Bobby said, "interior and exterior. In case you ever need it."

Mom shot me a look of disdain as if to say, *How dare you bring this loser to my table?* It wasn't hard to read her mind. I understood. Bobby didn't have a good job. In fact, he didn't have any job. Instead of discussing the elephant in the room, Mom regaled us with her knowledge of current events.

"Did you know those Cabbage Patch Dolls are the biggest toy again this Christmas?" Mom said. "I don't get it. They're not that cute."

* * *

I felt confident that Bobby's respectful behavior had won Mom and Dad over. No way could Mom complain—I hoped.

First thing the next morning, I called her to find out.

"So what do you think?" I asked.

"He looks half-dead," Mom answered.

Her nasty opinion stung me to my core.

"Mom, don't say that," I said. "Bobby's very much alive, and I'm in love with him. I think he's good-looking, don't you?"

Surely, she couldn't disagree with me on that point.

"Handsome is as handsome does," Mom said. "I smelled the alcohol on his breath."

"He's over twenty-one, Mom. Most people have a drink or two at Thanksgiving."

"You could do so much better," Mom said. "You need to marry someone who can take care of you financially, like your sister did."

"Money isn't everything," I said.

"Maybe not," she said, "but having money makes life a lot easier. What if you marry him and have kids? What happens when one of them gets sick? Come on, Susan, wake up."

I shook my head. I didn't know what to say. I wouldn't allow myself to look at the sacrifices I'd have to make to stay with Bobby. Instead, I spent the next three years making excuses for his bad behavior and pretending Bobby'd make a great husband and father. I only had to love him enough to make him see his true potential. It never occurred to me that he wouldn't want to change for me.

Besides, if Mom and Dad wanted me to marry someone with money, they sure hadn't set me up for success. With that goal in mind, they should've christened me a debutante or at least sent me to etiquette school so I'd know how to behave correctly around the wealthy. I didn't even know which fork to use at a fancy dinner party.

* * *

Bobby and I celebrated our first New Year's Eve as a couple. We welcomed 1987 together, watching the ball drop in Times Square on TV.

"Three, two, one! Happy New Year!"

"Get over here, babe." Bobby took my face in his hands and planted a tender kiss on my lips.

I finally had a boyfriend to kiss at midnight.

"I've been thinking about my dad since Thanksgiving. It's time I find him."

"I'm proud of you, Bobby," I said. "That's so brave. Can I help?"

"No, I've got to do this on my own."

On New Year's day, Bobby left on his quest to find his father. He traveled to who knows where while I brought Blondie with me for dinner with my folks.

"Glad you didn't bring that Bobby character with you," Mom smirked. "Why can't you find a successful guy for once?"

"Bobby's successful." I lost my appetite and put my fork down. "You should let him paint your house." I got an empty feeling in the pit of my stomach.

11. Lady and the Tramp

I chose to look at Bobby through the proverbial rose-colored glasses.

"What's wrong with you, Susan?" Dad sat back and crossed his arms. "We taught you better."

"What can I say? I love the guy."

Mom's and Dad's scathing words gave me a stomachache. I almost had to pull over on the way home to throw up. Thankfully, I made it back without incident and took some Maalox to settle my rumbling tummy.

Blondie and I relaxed on the couch, watching one of my all-time favorite television specials, *A Charlie Brown Christmas*. Peppermint Patty had just invited herself to Charlie Brown's house for the holiday when Bobby returned, a look of total defeat on his face. He slumped on the couch next to me. I turned off the television to give him my full attention.

"I found his last wife," Bobby said, "at least, the last one I knew about. But they're divorced, and she doesn't know where my dad is. Her kid looked exactly like me."

"That's your half-brother, Bobby."

"I know," Bobby said. "One of many. Dad married six different women. My guess is, he already left number seven and is with his eighth, maybe ninth, by now."

Poor, poor Bobby. I'd thought my family had problems. The Hartzlers looked healthy in comparison.

* * *

Bobby and I settled into a comfortable routine—me climbing the career ladder, Bobby spending his days with Blondie at my apartment. I liked being part of a couple even if our coupling didn't meet my parents' standards.

On our second Christmas Eve together, I got off work early to celebrate with my man and my dog. Besides decorating our tiny apartment with blinking lights and hanging Christmas bulbs from the ceiling, I planned a romantic evening. We'd enjoy a candlelit dinner accompanied by a case of beer. Oh, holy night.

Bobby greeted me with his tongue sticking out.

"What's wrong with you?"

"I don't know," Bobby garbled. "My tongue's stiff. Started this afternoon."

I thought maybe Bobby suffered from holiday stress. He tended to

Peace on Earth Goodwill to all ~~Men~~ ~~Women~~ Dogs

Love, Blondie and Susan

A Christmas card from me and Blondie (photograph by Susanne Hayek).

be a hypochondriac anyway. I didn't know whether to laugh or cry; he looked so silly.

"Did you eat something weird?" I asked. "Maybe it's an allergic reaction."

"Maybe," he murmured.

"You need to see a doctor."

"No," Bobby muddled. "Can't. No insurance."

"Did you ingest some paint?"

Bobby ignored me.

Within an hour, his arms stiffened too.

"I'm taking you to the hospital," I said.

This time, Bobby didn't argue.

"Take me to County," Bobby tried to tell me.

I helped him to my car. We hit no traffic that night. I assumed everyone was home, enjoying their Christmas dinner with family and friends. Not me and Bobby.

The LAC + USC Medical Center, referred to as County, was packed, though, even on Christmas Eve. At check-in, Bobby held himself up by leaning against a counter until he passed out right there in the waiting room, convulsing and shaking.

Two nurses went into action. They laid him on his back and put his legs up on a chair above his heart level.

"Get a gurney, stat," one of the nurses yelled while another performed CPR.

"Is he diabetic?" someone asked in a shrill voice. "Did he recently suffer a head injury?"

"He hit his head last night." I remembered Bobby's fall when we'd left his friend's Christmas party the night before.

"Could be swelling on the brain," the nurse yelled as they lifted him to the gurney.

Bobby, now conscious, looked like a frightened little boy lying there, helpless, tears in his eyes.

I love you, he mouthed through his oxygen mask.

"I love you too." I didn't realize I was confusing pity with love.

"You stay here," a nurse told me.

I watched her wheel Bobby away into one of the emergency center's makeshift rooms.

"We'll let you know when we find out what's wrong."

The only seat available in the crowded waiting room was next to a putrid-smelling homeless man. The man's clothes were so tattered that his big toes stuck out of his shoes. My attention was averted when the emergency team sprang into action again to help the victim of a car accident. I pressed my palm over my lips when I saw all the blood.

Finally, a doctor approached me. "He might have lockjaw," he said. "We think he stepped on a rusty nail. He works in construction, right?"

"He paints houses from time to time," I said, "but not recently."

"We'll run some more tests." The doctor disappeared in a hurry down the hall.

I thought about calling someone, but by then, the time was near midnight. Anyway, there was a long line at the pay phone. So, I sat there, alone, gulping down my breath. How I wished Blondie were allowed in the hospital.

Bobby's doctor came back a short time later and said, "It's not lockjaw. We're admitting him. He's had an accidental overdose."

"Overdose?" I stepped back. "From what?"

"We don't know," the doctor said. "Bobby can't reach the friend who gave him the pills. Whatever they were, he took enough to die. He's resting now. We gave him something to sleep. He'll be fine. You can see him tomorrow."

On my way home, I couldn't get that stupid cliché *What's a nice girl like you doing in a place like this?* to stop playing in my head. Then, I remembered last night's party. The more I thought about that weird soiree, the stranger it seemed.

One of Bobby's best friends, Jeff, had decided to celebrate the season at a rehab facility in Santa Monica. Jeff wasn't a patient there. He worked as an orderly at the longterm-care facility. Bobby and I thought the whole thing was hilarious, Jeff throwing a party there. Who would party at a rehab?

*   *   *

Blondie tried her best to console me. She did her happy dance to welcome me home and tried to kiss my tears away, but nothing worked. I tossed and turned all night.

First thing the next morning, I rushed to the hospital.

Bobby looked like a ghost in his hospital bed. So pale. The love of my life was in a psych ward. His doctor put him on a psych hold. He looked so tiny in his hospital bed surrounded by machines that beeped and buzzed, with occasional screams from other patients that echoed though the hall.

"Oh, Bobby," I said.

His roommate let out what sounded like a growl. I jumped.

"Don't worry about him, babe. He's harmless. Thinks he's a tiger."

"Bobby, you could've died," I said.

"Don't be so dramatic," Bobby said. "I'm fine."

My heart skipped a beat when I heard a crash in the hall. Nurses quickly ran past the room.

"Ignore that," Bobby said. "Happens all the time around here."

"What's with the pills?" I pinched my lips tight.

"Something Jeff gives patients when they're convulsing," Bobby said. "I took one when we got home, but it didn't do anything. So I took a few more."

"A few more?" I said. "Bobby, what in the hell were you thinking?"

"I wanted to get high, that's all."

"I know you drink too much," I said, "but when did you start taking pills?"

"I know," he said. "I've learned my lesson. I can't be around any pills—ever."

"You doctor told me you need help." My stomach churned.

"Don't fuckin' nag me."

"I'm sorry," I said. "I didn't mean it to come out that way. I care about you. Don't want to see you go through anything like this again."

"You think I want to repeat this nightmare? Imagine waking up in the psych ward on Christmas Day to a guy dressed like Santa. He gave me a toothbrush, gift wrapped with a tube of toothpaste."

"At least you got a visit from Santa."

"What I really want is a candy bar," Bobby said, rearranging his pillows. "Got any cash? There's a vending machine on this floor."

"Where? I'll get one for you before I leave."

I related to Bobby's sweet tooth. I craved some chocolate myself at that moment. Chocolate could fix anything, except for this. Bobby needed a lot more than sugar.

"No, no," Bobby said. "I want to get out of this bed and walk around a bit."

I picked up my purse and pulled out my wallet. "All I've got is five dollars. Want that?"

He nodded and took it.

"I'll come check on you later," I said, "after dinner with my folks."

"Tell them I said Merry Christmas," Bobby said.

I gave him a kiss and walked out.

By the time I put my key in the ignition, I realized how much I was shaking. *Was Bobby a drug addict too?* I needed Angel.

12

Bite Me

I headed home, picked up Blondie, and went straight to Angel's. Bobby and I had planned to stop by her house anyway before an early Christmas dinner with my parents.

I stared down at Blondie before ringing the doorbell. She wagged her tail, completely oblivious to my racing heart. The thought of breaking Mom's rule and sharing something this colossal put chills down my spine. She didn't want anyone outside the five of us to know about any hardship. It's hard to believe Mom's critical words still echoed in my head, scolding me even throughout my adulthood. The worst part, I'd allowed that to happen.

Angel's dogs must have smelled us because they sounded the alarm. Blondie scratched at the door, eager to play with her pack.

With the chain guard on, Angel peeked out. "Darling, it's you," she said in a bubbly voice.

She stepped aside to let Blondie dart past. I couldn't move.

"Are you okay?" Her perky tone changed. "Where's Bobby?"

"That's what I wanted to talk to you about." I fell into Angel's arms and cried. "I ... think Bobby's a d-drug addict." My lips trembled. "He's in the hos-p-pital."

"Calm down, sweetikins." Angel wiped her hands on her holiday apron and gently pulled me inside. "Tell me what happened."

I sighed, "He overdosed. I don't know what to do."

The dam burst inside me. Tears streamed down my face.

"Was Bobby trying to kill himself?" Angel asked.

"No, he took too many of whatever pills he had gotten his hands on. They're calling it an accidental overdose. I don't mean to lay this on you, especially on Christmas, but I don't have anyone else to talk to."

Angel guided me to the living room. We passed her giant Christmas tree. The mere sight of the angel that topped her tree made me cry even more. When we reached her posh suede couch, Angel helped me sit down.

"John and the girls are at the park," Angel said. "They won't be home for about an hour. Talk to me."

"I've tried my best to show Bobby I love him." My whole body shook. "I believed in him, nurtured his creativity, thought I could take away his pain."

I held my head in my hands and shook my head.

"Is he okay?" Angel asked.

"He seemed okay this morning. As good as anyone would be after spending the night in the psych ward."

Angel put her arm around me. "What did he take?"

"He doesn't even know," I said, sobbing. "Some friend of his gave him p-pills. Now, that friend's MIA."

"Everything's going to be okay." Angel cradled me in her arms. "You'll get past this. And Bobby too."

I should've known Bobby's behavior wouldn't shock Angel. She'd seen it all, hanging out with Andy Warhol at The Factory in the late '60s, a haven for drugs and sex.

Blondie and the pack came charging into the room. They zipped past us, stopping only to roll around with the occasional bark and nip. If only I could trade places with my dog. As the saying went, ignorance was bliss.

"I'm worried about you." Angel looked directly into my eyes. "Did you take anything?"

"No," I said. "I didn't even know he had. I rushed him to the hospital and watched him pass out in front of me. He could have died."

"I can't even imagine," Angel said. "If John ever did that to me, I'd kill him."

"And now, I have to go to my parents' and act like nothing's wrong," I said, sobbing.

Angel wiped away my tears. "You didn't cause this. Bobby took the pills."

"I know, but he's my boyfriend." I shrugged. "Guilty by association."

"You're not culpable," Angel said. "But what are you afraid of?"

"That Mom and Dad will find out what a horrible person I am."

"How does Bobby's bad behavior make you a horrible person?" Angel leaned back and looked me in the eyes.

"They warned me about dating him. I feel so stupid."

"Listen, everyone makes mistakes," Angel said. "You, me, Bobby, your mother, and your father. We are all perfectly imperfect in God's eyes. Trust me. You'll become stronger, having lived through this. I promise."

"I don't think I can take any more strength training," I said, "if this is what I have to go through."

"Here." She gave me a box of Kleenex. "How long will he be in the hospital?"

"He's on a seventy-two-hour hold," I answered and wiped my face. "I feel like I'm having an out-of-body experience. Me, dating someone on a psych hold. How the hell did that happen?"

Angel took my hands in hers. "Darling, you know I'm always here for you."

I felt my eyes well up with tears again.

"So I'm going to say this. Again. The time has come for you to see a therapist."

I nodded my head in agreement. I knew I had to do something.

"Do you still have the number I gave you?" she asked.

"Yeah, I put it in a safe place. I promise, I'll call her. But before I can do anything, I've got to get through this damn dinner. I can't tell Mom and Dad what happened. They'd never forgive me."

"But you did nothing wrong," Angel reiterated.

I nodded, feeling light-headed. "How can I sit there and act like this didn't happen."

"First off, let's clean your face." She stood and led me down that long hall to her bathroom, the place she called The Religious Room.

I looked around at all the Catholic art and crosses she'd hung and considered her words.

"We are all perfectly imperfect."

I saw my reflection in the mirror. "Jeez, what a mess. I look like something out of a horror flick."

Streaks of black ran down my cheeks from mascara.

Angel took a jar of Vaseline from a cupboard along with some cotton balls.

"There's nothing wrong with crying," she said. "You've got to get your feelings out." She carefully cleaned away the ugly black streaks. "There, that's better."

"I wish you could clean last night away." I wiped my nose.

"Me too." Angel hugged me good-bye.

*   *   *

I turned to my faithful copilot on the way to the Valley.

12. Bite Me

"You've got to help me though this," I said to Blondie in the car. She licked my cheek.

"Thank you, girlie girl. I love you too."

I didn't turn on the radio. I needed silence to gather my thoughts before I put on my best happy face.

Breathe, Susan, just breathe.

My entire body tightened when I found Mom in the kitchen, cooking. Working in the kitchen always made her irritable even though she was an expert cook. Her negative attitude made holidays especially stressful for the entire family.

"Help me with this," she said and tossed me an oven mitt.

The two of us took the turkey out of the oven and set the roasting pan on the counter. We carefully placed the bird on a turkey platter. Blondie followed me, licking her lips, while I carried the turkey to the dining room where Dad would do the carving.

"Don't let me forget the biscuits," Mom said. "I don't want to burn them again this year."

I cleared my throat and nodded. Deep inside, I worried I wouldn't remember. I had to concentrate on keeping my secret.

"Get the good china," Mom snapped. "Your grandmother's silverware too."

"Sure," I said, "but there's only three of us."

"Where is Bobby? Did you finally come to your senses?"

"No, Mom," I said, setting three plates to the white linen tablecloth. "Bobby and I are still very much in love."

After I set the table, I helped Mom bring out her mashed potatoes made with heaps of butter, simple boiled onions, her famous green bean casserole, fresh cranberry sauce, rich gravy made from browned scrapings at the bottom of the turkey roasting pan, and the *pièce de résistance*—her classic sage stuffing. She'd also baked an apple pie for dessert.

"Go get your father," Mom said. "Dinner's ready."

I went out back to find Dad raking leaves. Blondie jumped into his pile. Leaves scattered all over the lawn again.

"Don't do that, girlie," I scolded her. "I can help you with that after we eat," I told him, trying my best to keep everything calm.

He put his rake down and hugged me. Dad's strong arms around me made me feel safe, like I could tell him the truth. But I didn't.

When Dad followed me inside, we were welcomed by the smell of something burning.

73

"Darn it, Susan," Mom said. "I told you to remind me to take the biscuits out."

"I'm sorry."

I wanted to cry, wanted to tell Mom what had happened to Bobby. Maybe then she'd lighten up on me. But I couldn't.

Silence permeated the room while the three of us sat there, eating. I took a few bites but had a hard time swallowing any food, my stomach flip-flopping.

Blondie sat at my feet under the table, waiting for me to share my dinner with her. I had lots of experience in that regard. My childhood dog, Siesta, never ate a can of dog food her entire life. She'd lived off my table scraps along with bologna and the occasional doughnut. A wonder how she'd lived twenty-one years.

"How's work going?" Dad asked, ignoring the fact that Bobby was a no-show.

"Good," I answered. "I got a new client, the Fund for Animals. We're working on getting an anti-vivisection law passed."

"What's that?" Mom asked between bites.

"My client is committed to putting an end to the use of live animals in medical research," I explained, happy to talk about anything but Bobby. "Some of the animals they use are from the pound." I looked at Blondie, drooling under the table. "Could you imagine my Blondie being used for research?"

Our Christmas dinner was interrupted by the doorbell.

"I'll get it," I said, happy to have a few moments away from the table.

I opened the door to see Bobby standing in front of me.

"Hi, babe." He wore the same jeans and T-shirt he'd had on the night before.

I pressed my hands against my cheeks. "What are you doing here?"

"They let me out," he said.

I found out later that he'd escaped from his psych hold. Bobby had used the candy money I had given him for the bus.

Before I could say anything, Bobby threw his arms around me and hugged me tight. I didn't reciprocate; I stood frozen.

"Thanks for being there for me," he said. "I couldn't have gotten through that whole ordeal without you."

We walked into the dining room.

"Look who made it," I announced with a forced smile.

"Ho, ho, ho. Merry Christmas," Dad welcomed Bobby. "Grab a seat."

"Susan will fix you a plate," Mom said with a smirk. "Sorry, but we don't have any biscuits. Susan burned them."

Bobby sat down and filled his plate. His hands shook with every bite. Some of his food fell off the fork before he could get it in his mouth. I saw Mom had noticed too. She turned away and changed the subject.

"Did you hear about our vice president's Christmas cards disaster?" Mom pushed her sleeves up. "That stupid Dan Quayle sent three thousand cards out with word beacon spelled B-E-A-K-O-N. It's a wonder anything gets done in Washington, D.C., these days."

"If only everyone in the world consulted with you, Mom, then no one would ever make another mistake."

"That's right," Mom said, her face beaming. "And don't you forget it."

I looked across the table at my big mistake—Bobby—and wondered what Mom would say if she knew about last night. I wasn't planning on staying around to find out.

* * *

Bobby turned his whole body toward me on our car ride home. His intense stare made me feel uncomfortable. I looked at Blondie through my rearview mirror. How I'd rather have her sitting next to me in the passenger seat.

I pouted, keeping my hands on the wheel at ten and two and my eyes on the road.

"Last night ... that was my bottom," he said. "It's all up from here, babe. I promise. For me and you. And Blondie too."

"Can't get much worse." My chest tightened.

"You're so good to me." Bobby covered his face with his hands and cried. "I can't lose you, please. Give me another chance. You'll see. I'll get better."

"No more drugs," I said, my shoulders back, my eyes still on the road. "And no more drinking either. Got it?"

"I swear. I'll give up everything."

"You scared me."

"I know. I'm sorry I put you and Blondie though that." He reached his hand to pet Blondie in the backseat. "I've learned my lesson. The new me starts now."

"You really mean it?" My mood lifted.

"Absolutely," Bobby said. "To prove it, I want you to drop me off at Cedars. I'm going to a meeting."

"What meeting?" I asked. "You have a meeting on Christmas?"

"AA, babe," Bobby said. "You know, Alcoholics Anonymous? They've got meetings every day of the year. I arranged to have a friend bring me home after."

I took one hand off the steering wheel and squeezed Bobby's knee. "Just get sober. That's the only present I need."

13

Pawtograph

Bobby stopped drinking. He attended AA meetings daily and even got himself a sponsor. I learned all about the Twelve Steps, the guiding principles that outline a course of action for tackling addiction problems. Bobby's about-face inspired me to join Al-Anon, the program of recovery for the families and friends of alcoholics.

At first, I felt like an impostor in Al-Anon. I'd hear story after story about drunken, violent parents causing absolutely horrific childhoods. My mom and dad seemed ideal in comparison. They never drank. The most I had to complain about was not having a color TV or a swimming pool.

Following the Twelve Steps made life peaceful for Bobby and me. Even Blondie held her feathered tail high again. No more drama. Still, I had major concerns about the movie premiere I had to work the following week. My job at movie premieres? To find celebrities and deliver them to the *Entertainment Tonight* crew for interviews. Bobby loved to be my date at these exclusive events, but I worried about his sobriety amid the free-flowing booze.

"I heard in a meeting that staying away from alcohol is imperative in AA," I said. "Maybe you'd better sit this one out."

"I can be around it," Bobby said, "I just can't drink any."

Bobby and I arrived at the Beverly Hills Hotel for the premiere of *Cinema Paradiso*, an Italian flick that everyone in Hollywood was raving about. In fact, the enchanting story of a young boy's lifelong love affair with the movies won the Academy Award for Best Foreign Language Film in 1990.

The hotel ballroom was transformed into a quaint Italian village, complete with twinkling lights and live olive trees. I was stationed by the door to catch stars as they arrived. The famous and not-so-famous showed up within minutes.

"You can stay here and help me," I said to Bobby. That way, I could keep my eye on him and make sure he didn't drink. "You're so good at recognizing famous faces."

"Don't worry, babe. I'll be fine." He turned and got lost in the crowd.

Shortly after Bobby left, I spotted Kevin Bacon. He entered the ballroom, surrounded by his entourage.

"Kevin." I squeezed through his posse to grab his hand. "Come with me."

"Who are you?" he asked.

"I'm Susan Hartzler," I said like he should recognize my name. Before Kevin could react, I pulled him away from his friends and delivered the star to the *ET* crew set up in a quiet-ish corner.

On the way back, I scanned the crowded room. That was when I noticed Bobby with a drink.

He held out his glass to toast newlyweds Tom Cruise and Mimi Rogers.

"Shit," I muttered to myself. Just when things were going so well.

The sight of him with a cocktail made me feel ill.

I stuffed my feelings and got back to work, stopping Sally Field and delivering her to the *ET* crew.

The party raged. I worried. But along came Jack Nicholson. I dragged the actor off to be interviewed.

Celeb after celeb, I stopped them in their tracks. Then, I remembered seeing Bobby with that drink.

When I found him, Bobby was holding court with a crowd of wanna-bes hanging on his every word. I tapped him on the shoulder. He turned to me with that stupid devilish grin, a telltale sign that he'd had a few drinks. *Oh no, not again.*

Bobby put his arm around me and said, "I was just talking about you."

A tall, slim, red-headed woman sidled up next to me. "Your boyfriend told us all about you," she said, "how you saved his life."

Oh jeez. Bobby told all these people about that? He admitted being in a psych ward?

I pursed my lips when Bobby held up his glass to toast me.

"To my hero," he said.

I rolled my eyes and pulled Bobby away. "What are you doing?" I asked, pointing at his drink.

"It's Pepsi, babe. Why would I blow my sobriety now? Just got my ninety-day chip." He patted his jeans pocket where he kept his treasured chip.

"Why the hell would you tell those strangers what happened to you?"

13. Pawtograph

"I said I almost died from an allergic reaction, left out the part about taking pills."

"Let's get real here," I said. "The doctor called it an accidental overdose. You took a lethal dose of whatever your friend had given you."

Bobby put his drink down on a nearby table, grabbed my hands and placed his forehead on mine. "I'm sorry, babe. I thought it was cool to tell them what a lifesaver you are to me. I didn't mean to minimize what happened."

Right there in the middle of the party chaos, I pulled Bobby into me and gave him a big kiss.

* * *

Bobby handed me a fresh cup of coffee one morning. Since getting sober, he got out of bed with me to make my coffee, just like he had when we first got together.

"Can I borrow your car today?" Bobby asked. "I'm going to sign up with Central Casting. Figured I can get some work as an extra until my music career takes off."

"That's an excellent idea." I winked. "Of course you can borrow my car. I don't have any meetings outside the office today anyway."

I'd heard in Al-Anon that my support would only enhance Bobby's chances of success in his program. *How's that for support?* If I could have, I would have patted myself on the back.

"Once things get going, I'll be able to help with the bills," Bobby said. "And who knows? Maybe I'll get discovered."

Bobby pitching in to help me pay the bills? Woohoo!

"I'm so proud of you and happy for me. It'll be a big relief to have some help."

Bobby brought Blondie in the car to drop me off at work. He promised to take her home after a quick walk and then head straight to Central Casting.

"No work as an extra for little Miss Blondie."

"Darn," I said. "With her movie-star good looks, you'd think casting directors would be all over her."

"Imagine if she got discovered," Bobby said.

"She's already a superstar in my eyes. But if she became the next Lassie, I suppose I'd have to get busy helping her sign pawtographs." I giggled and gave Blondie a kiss on the nose. "Have a good time, you two," I shouted and watched Bobby speed away in my car.

I wanted to spend the entire day looking out the window of my office to daydream about my future. But I couldn't. I had a press conference to prepare for—my first ever—for my favorite client, the Fund for Animals. Me, promoting an animal charity? My boyfriend now sober? Could life get any better than that?

I booked one of the meeting rooms at the landmark nineteen-story Century Plaza Hotel for the upcoming press conference. The property, in the heart of Century City, had earned an impeccable reputation for hosting celebrities, foreign dignitaries, and presidents, including Ronald Reagan. While Ronald Reagan had been in office, he'd stayed in the hotel's tower so frequently that the media dubbed it his Western White House. Good enough for Ronnie, good enough to promote saving the lives of countless pets.

I shared the good news with my client during our weekly conference call. Animal advocate Gretchen Wyler served as vice chairperson for the Fund for Animals, now an affiliate of the mega animal rights group, the Humane Society of the United States.

"The Century Plaza is perfect," Gretchen said, "centrally located and well known by the media. Good job. I have three doctors confirmed to speak."

"You'll speak, too, right?" I asked.

"Of course. I'll act as the moderator," Gretchen answered. "You take care of logistics and get the media there. I'll do the rest."

Gretchen had hired the public relations firm I worked for to promote a Senate bill she'd helped create, calling for an end to the use of pound animals in medical research. Once passed, Gretchen's bill would make the practice illegal in the state of California. After we achieved that goal, the actress-turned-crusader planned to take her cause nationwide.

When our conference call ended, I sat back and stared at the jacaranda tree outside my office window, imagining Bobby and me standing underneath it in the middle of a field of purple lupine. Of course, Blondie stood by my side, a big white satin bow on her head. In my mind's eye, I watched the three of us standing with a justice of the peace, the tree's lavender blooms gracefully falling around us.

Back to reality. With so much to get done for the press conference, I had to pull myself together and get down to business.

I took out the company's *Bacon's Media Directory* to create a tailored list of press to invite. Searching though volumes of gigantic, heavy books was tedious, but it had to be done in order to find updated contact information.

After scouring through several volumes, I typed the names and addresses to envelopes and added the necessary twenty-five-cent stamp. Next, I wrote a media alert with all the details, copied it, and then stuffed the copies into envelopes. I'd drop off the bundle at the post office on the way home.

As promised, Bobby showed up at the end of my workday. He waited patiently for me in the parking lot.

"Hey, babe," he said. "How was work?"

Blondie wiggled and wagged in the backseat. "Good. Very busy. Got a lot accomplished. How did your day go?"

"Excellent," Bobby said, placing a magazine in my hand, opened to an article about a dog audition.

"What's this?" I asked.

"Blondie's big break," Bobby said, his shoulders back.

"*An open call for canine actors*," I read out loud. "Says *trained dogs*. Blondie won't even sit on command."

"So what?" Bobby said. "She might be exactly what they're looking for, babe. I can see it now. You and Blondie on *Oprah*."

I laughed. "Making a living, spending time with Blondie...."

"Her long blonde hair and that confident strut," Bobby said. "Anyone would want Blondie as their spokesdog, don't ya think?"

I looked at Blondie now curled up in the back. "She is pretty cute, but I'm her owner. Do you really think she could be an actress?"

"Abso-fucking-lutely."

Bobby's enthusiasm was hard to resist.

"I guess I could take the day off," I said, "and see how she does."

"You'll never know unless you try."

"Time for your close-up, girlie girl," I put my hand in the backseat. "It's unanimous. Blondie just licked me in agreement."

I remembered when Bobby had hit bottom, he'd told that our life would be up from there. Boy, did he get that right.

* * *

Blondie and I arrived at the doggie audition in Hollywood and took our place at the end of a long line of trainers and their dogs. None of the other trainers seemed particularly interested in meeting either one of us. I fidgeted, picked at my cuticles, twirled my hair, psyched myself into a frenzy. Blondie didn't care. She lay down on the dead grass outside the run-down warehouse where the auditions would take place, content to spend time with me.

I realized I hadn't thought this through when I observed the professional handlers' array of training paraphernalia. I'd only brought my dog.

I watched as they took their well-trained dogs out of their crates and put them through some exercises to prepare for the audition. I, on the other hand, kept Blondie on a leash and allowed her to pull me around while I struggled to keep our place in line.

Still, I felt extremely confident that Blondie had a good shot at getting the gig. To me, she was by far the prettiest canine in line. I imagined her as the poster dog for shelter animals nationwide. We'd visit pounds across the country, encouraging people to rescue.

"Lady, lady!"

I snapped out of my daydream to find a strange man standing in front of me.

"You're up. Follow me."

I followed the man into a dark warehouse. Stage lights illuminated a living room set. The only other light crept through dirty windows that outlined the space. Through the dim lighting, I saw a long table where the casting team sat.

"Stand there." The man pointed to a red × on the floor.

Blondie pulled me in the opposite direction, toward a comfy-looking couch. But I yanked her back, firmly held her leash, and waited for instructions.

"Name?" someone yelled from behind the casting table.

"I'm Susan, and this is Blondie."

She turned to look at me.

"Isn't she the most beautiful dog?"

That was when I noticed her fluffy backside faced the decision-makers. I tried to get her to turn around, but she wouldn't budge. She just stood there, staring at me, her pink tongue hanging out of her mouth.

Another casting agent said, "Put her in a down-stay and have her cover her eyes with her paws."

Dumbfounded, I tried to figure out how to get Blondie to do what they'd asked.

"Sit," I said.

Blondie looked up at me and wagged her tail. I tried to telepathically get her to cover her eyes with her paws. She licked her chops and tried to pull me over to that comfy-looking couch.

"Down," I said.

Blondie stood motionless.

"Well, can she do anything?" someone else on the casting team asked.

"How about I attach wires to her paws and maneuver them off camera?" I answered. "Not really," I said, "but look at this face." I took Blondie's head in my hands and turned her snout toward the decision-makers.

"You brought a dog here, not a puppet. Next!"

In the car on the way home, I replayed the scene in my mind. *Did I really believe that Blondie would magically become a movie star?*

"What was I thinking?" I asked the moment I walked through the door.

"I take it Blondie didn't get the gig." Bobby bent down and kissed Blondie.

"No," I answered. "She didn't. And I made a complete fool of myself."

"It's okay." Bobby put his arms around me and hugged me tight. "Remember step one. *You are powerless.*" He lifted my chin and planted a soft kiss on my mouth. "In my eyes, you succeeded just by trying."

"I guess so," I said. "Why is this all so hard?"

"No one said life was easy."

"When did you become such a philosopher?" I asked, happy to see my man in such high spirits.

"It's the program, babe. I'm working my program."

14

Working Like a Dog

I woke up early the next morning to make a final round of calls to the media. When I finished contacting practically every outlet in Los Angeles, I felt confident the event would be a huge success. To make sure, I headed directly to the Century Plaza. I didn't want to leave anything to chance.

I left my car with the valet and headed to Conference Room A. The coffee and tea station we'd ordered was already set up. My mouth watered when I eyed the assortment of pastries, which included chocolate croissants. But I resisted. I could indulge later.

I headed to the podium to add a sign that read *Physicians for Pets*, a clever way to get the media's respect. Otherwise, some of the journalists might think the bill was part of a scheme cooked up by some crazy animal fanatics.

I felt a tap on my shoulder.

"There you are, Susan," Gretchen said. "What media's confirmed?"

For some reason, my mind went completely blank. "Uh, er...," I stammered. I looked up, hoping a bolt of lightning would strike and illuminate my brain but it didn't. After a few tense moments, a switch turned on in my head. I had prepared for this possibility with my trusty notepad.

"Let me see." I scanned my notes. "KABC, KCBS, KNBC—all confirmed. So did the *Los Angeles Times*." Not bad. Three of the top local TV news stations and the town's most prestigious paper.

"NPR's not coming?" Gretchen asked. "What about the AP? Or any of the other syndicates?"

I swallowed hard and opened my mouth to say something but thought better of it.

She continued, "What about the other local television stations? We need to get as much press as possible. The unnecessary suffering of innocent dogs and cats must stop."

Nothing like laying life or death on me minutes before the event began. "I'll make another round of calls."

On my way to the pay phone, I saw the crew from KABC enter the room. My head throbbed. *What's my priority? Should I show the crew where to set up or make last-minute calls like the client requested?*

I decided to do both. I'd get the crew settled first and then head to the pay phone.

Only, by the time I showed the cameraman where to plug in his microphone, another television crew arrived. Then another and another. My attention pulled this way and that. My heart pounded, and my mouth was dry.

I never made it to the pay phone. But it turned out, I hadn't needed to. The room was filled with press; it looked like every media outlet in town had shown up. I welcomed them with an updated press release that included facts about the bill that Gretchen had developed with California senator David Roberti, one of the Golden State's most prominent lawmakers.

Before I knew it, Gretchen was standing at the podium, and she began speaking. The senator couldn't fit the press conference into his busy schedule, but the three doctors Gretchen had convinced to support her bill stood by the podium, waiting to be introduced. These were well-known professionals with respected careers. One was an esteemed heart surgeon, the second was a leading oncologist, and the third was a celebrity plastic surgeon. All were on board to stand up for defenseless animals with the facts to support their expert opinions.

It didn't surprise me that my client had gotten the best to back her. Gretchen had a manner that could convince anyone to see things her way, especially when it came to animals. Word was that, at one time, she'd persuaded Zsa Zsa Gabor to burn all her mink coats.

I listened to the oncologist.

"The reason I'm against animal research is because it doesn't work," he said. "In fact, I believe it has no scientific value. Every scientist I have discussed the issue with agrees."

The heart surgeon added, "Almost all animal experiments are indefensible. All you have to do is look at the issue from a statistical, scientific basis to realize there is no validity or reliability when it comes to this practice."

"Vivisection is barbaric and useless," the plastic surgeon added. "The best way to learn how to operate is from other surgeons. In fact, it's the only way, and every good surgeon knows that."

I was proud to be part of the dedicated team calling for an end to this terrible practice and hoped the media would cover the story fairly. Looking around at the sea of news crews and reporters made me sigh with relief. The press conference had turned out way better than I could have imagined.

Maybe my success had to do with my Twelve Step program. I thought about step one; we admitted we were powerless over alcohol— our lives had become unmanageable. I replaced the word *alcohol* with *press conference*, and it struck me. Letting go of the things I couldn't control might be the key to succeeding in every aspect of my life. Perhaps Bobby hitting rock bottom was the best thing to happen to me.

* * *

When I got home, I found my boyfriend busy in the kitchen, preparing dinner for me—cheese ravioli with fresh tomato and marinated artichoke hearts.

"Smells so good in here," I said, inhaling the spicy, sweet aroma of oregano.

"Taste this." He hand-fed me a spoonful of his homemade sauce. "I thought we'd celebrate your success."

"You're so sweet," I said. "But how'd you know I was successful?"

"I knew," Bobby said. "I just had a feeling you'd pull it off. Here, take a seat." He pulled out my chair.

"I have to admit, I got through the day, thanks to my program. Those steps really make a difference."

"Cool, babe," he said. "The steps are working for me too. Central Casting called with my first extra job. Got a six a.m. call time tomorrow. I need the car."

"Of course," I said. "I'll grab a cab."

In my effort to support Bobby, I forgot about my own needs. He needed my car, so I had to pay to get my butt to work.

I'd heard the term *enabling* in a meeting, but I didn't fully understand it. Despite good intentions, enablers like me could stand in between an addict and their recovery and were usually unaware of the negative effect they had. Not good for the addict, and not good for the enabler, either. One thing was sure; enabling came naturally to me. It made me feel good to help others. Since I had been a little girl, I'd always received praise for it. Looked like I'd have to work hard to change that.

* * *

14. Working Like a Dog

I woke Bobby at four the next morning.

"Go away," he said and rolled over.

"Come on, sleeping beauty. You've got work today, remember?"

I watched Bobby drag himself out of bed and prepare for his Hollywood debut.

"Good luck today."

"Leave me alone," he said, tying his shoe.

I let his snarky attitude go, figuring he had angst about his first day at work. When I heard the door slam behind him, I went back to sleep until my alarm went off at seven. I quietly got ready for work and called a cab.

* * *

After a long day at the office, I couldn't wait to get home and put my feet up. Maybe Bobby would be back already too. If so, we could order a pizza.

"Hi," Bobby greeted me, beer in hand. "I nailed it. They loved me."

The sight of him drinking again made my stomach churn. I'd taken his verbal insults and lies in stride; nursed him back to health after his drug overdose; put up with his erratic mood swings, extreme narcissism, and cleaning obsession; and paid for everything. No more!

"What the hell?" I said, my heart pounding, my hands shaking. "I thought you quit drinking."

"I did," he slurred. "I'm celebrating. A job well done. They want me back tomorrow, so I'll need the car again."

He drained the rest of his beer in one swig.

"We have to talk."

Bobby grabbed another beer. "Want one?"

I ignored his ridiculous question. "This isn't working for me."

"What's not working for you?"

"Us," I said. "You and me."

"Whatcha talking about? I'm working, like you wanted."

I dropped my purse on the coffee table. Bobby picked it up and hung it on a hook he'd attached behind the door. My little apartment reminded me of that fake living room set. So spotless, as if no one lived there. I could see my reflection in the hardwood floor.

"Bobby," I said, hands on my hips. "What I need is a partner who pitches in, pulls his own weight, owns a car. I need more than just a clean floor."

I'm Not Single, I Have a Dog

"It's your fault things get so dirty around here," he said. "You leave your shit everywhere, and your dog sheds."

"Here's what needs to happen." I steadied my voice. "You'd better start looking for a new place to live. I'm done supporting you."

"Blondie'll miss me," he said. "I can't leave her."

She ran behind me, her tail between her legs.

"I love Blondie," Bobby said, "just don't like all the dirt she tracks in."

"What's your deal with dirt anyway?"

"You decide." He picked a blonde hair off my suit jacket. "What's better—clean or dirty?"

"You obviously believe clean is better," I said. "I'm not sure which I'd choose anymore. Since I met you, I keep making bad decisions."

Bobby hiccupped. "Somebody needs a little love."

When he grabbed me for a kiss, I smelled the beer and stale cigarettes on his breath. I recoiled and broke away from his embrace.

"What I need is you gone," I said. "You have to move out."

"So you want me to leave?" Bobby's nostrils flared like a rabid dog. "I've got news for you. I'm not going anywhere. Neither are you."

He looked more feral than human, his narrowed eyes bloodshot.

"You're scaring me," I said.

Bobby took a fighter's stance, guarding the front door. He forced me back every time I tried to get past. After several attempts, he pushed me so hard that I slipped on the floor. He yanked me up and put me in a chokehold. I could hardly breathe.

I managed to spit out, "Bobby, let me go!"

"You're not going anywhere, babe."

I struggled but couldn't get free.

Bobby dragged me to the bedroom and threw me onto the bed like a rag doll. On high alert, Blondie growled. Bobby kicked her away and slammed the bedroom door. I tried to get off the bed, but he shoved me back and straddled me, forcefully holding my arms and legs so I couldn't move.

He looked insane, like a wild animal, so I did what you were supposed to do when you were attacked by a bear in the woods. I played dead. I lay there motionless, wondering how I'd gotten there.

I stayed silent as tears ran down my face until he passed out on top of me. When I heard Bobby snore, I wiggled out from under him, grabbed Blondie and my car keys, and headed straight to Angel's house.

15

Barking Bad

Angel guided me from the hallway to her kitchen table. "He hurt you?" she asked, checking for marks on my neck. "Once a man gets violent, there's a good chance he'll do it again. You can't go home. Best if you stay here." She handed me a tea towel.

I wiped my tears, grateful to be with my friend. Angel's home felt like the safest place in the universe.

"John, the girls, and I only want the best for you," she said. "We love you."

"Love you guys, too, and I thought I loved Bobby, but his drinking frightens me."

"Alcoholism is no excuse for violence," Angel said. She put the kettle on to boil. "And it's not up to you to make him better. What's that line he's always quoting from AA?"

"'One day at a time'?"

She blew out a quick breath. "Seems like Bobby can't go one minute at a time. He's just not ready to stop drinking. But you don't have to take his abuse, sober or not." She laid her hands on the kitchen counter and stared directly into my eyes. "Please, call my therapist."

I nodded and bit my lip. "I should've called when you first suggested, but I had my reservations."

I flashed back to when my college sweetheart had broken up with me. It was a difficult time. I shared my concerns with Mom, hoping for some sage advice, reassurance, or, at least, an offer to pay for a therapy visit. But instead she'd reminded me that only crazy people saw therapists and that all I needed was to get out of bed and move on with life.

"Am I nuts?" I asked Angel, hoping to God she'd say no.

"No, darling, you're not nuts. You just need a little help, that's all."

"And you think therapy will help?"

"Absolutely. You'll learn what drew you to Bobby in the first place and figure out how to avoid making the same mistake in the future." She handed me a cup of chamomile tea. "Promise me you'll call this time."

"Okay, I'll call her tomorrow."

"Good," she said. "Meanwhile, you and Blondie can make yourselves comfortable here. I planned on asking you to stay here this summer anyway. Our house sitter called and canceled an hour ago."

I had known they were going somewhere, but my mind went blank. Angel smiled. "Remember, we're leaving for the Cape next week?"

"Oh, yeah, that's right. I totally forgot."

"That's understandable," she said. "Will you stay here all summer and look after things for us?"

"Of course."

"Call your landlord tonight and give notice," Angel continued. "Put your furniture in storage. That way you can take your time searching for a new place. We'll be back after Labor Day."

"Okay, that sounds like a good plan. Thanks," I said. "Just one problem." I pointed at the disheveled suit I'd had on since the press conference. "I have to work tomorrow, and I didn't bring anything with me."

She held up a hand in protest. "My closet's all yours."

"I couldn't—"

"You'll be doing me a favor," she cut in. "Consider it payment for walking our pups."

My eyes welled with tears. "Angel, I don't know what I'd do without you."

"I'm always here for you, darling," she said, giving me a warm hug. "You're family. Now, let's get you some pajamas."

*　　*　　*

I needed to focus on my job if that was at all possible. Even Angel's red Byblos pantsuit did little to make me feel better. But once I sat at my desk and got down to business, I started to breathe again. I got my jam back—until I saw Bobby headed my way, dripping in sweat. I figured he'd probably ridden here from my place on the bike I'd bought. I kept my cool, rose from my chair, and headed for the exit, motioning for him to follow. I couldn't handle any more of his drama, especially in my office.

I didn't stop until we were standing under the jacaranda tree in the parking lot—the same spot where I'd daydreamed about exchanging vows with Bobby. The parking lot was a perfect spot to tell him *adios* forever. At least I'd have witnesses if he tried to hurt me again.

"What are you doing here?" I asked.

He rubbed the back of his neck. "I'm sorry, babe. I'll never hurt you again."

"You're right, you won't."

"I'm sorry," he said. "What else can I say? You can't leave me. I'm afraid of what I'll do to myself if you leave me."

"Are you threatening suicide?"

"I can't live without you."

I stood firm, raised my hands—palms facing him—and said, "And I can't live with you. Look, I've had enough of your bullshit."

"I promise, I'll never hurt you again," he cried. "Please don't kick me out!"

I backed up a few steps. "Shit! All right, stay at my place until the end of the month. After that, you're on your own. I gave notice last night."

"Where are you going?" he asked, looking like a lost puppy.

"None of your business," I said and began walking back to the office. "I'll be coming to get my stuff next week."

"Babe," he cried out, running after me. "I'm begging you, give me another chance."

I spun around. "Bobby, I'm done. I need to get back to work."

* * *

Angel's therapist fit me into her schedule the following day. I liked her before we met in person, especially after she told me I could bring Blondie to my sessions.

Beverly worked out of an old Craftsman style house located a few miles from my office. The waiting area was more like a living room with fresh flowers and a worn leather couch. A door opened, and a woman in her sixties gestured for me to enter what used to be a bedroom, now her private office. She reminded me of a wise crone with her curly gray hair framing kind hazel eyes.

"Come in," she said, shaking my hand.

"I'm Susan, and this is...." I broke into tears, and she guided me to a comfy leather chair.

Blondie settled at my feet.

Beverly handed me a box of Kleenex and sat opposite us. "Why don't you tell me why you're here?"

"I rescued Blondie to keep me away from stupid guys, but I guess ... I need ... more than a dog," I cried. "There's something wrong with me. My boyfriend got violent, and it's all my fault...."

She waited until I caught my breath between sobs. I balled up a Kleenex in my hand, unable to speak. I didn't know how long I'd been sitting there, crying, but it was long enough to realize that listening to me was something Mom never did.

"What did he do to you?" Beverly asked.

"We argued, and he forced me onto the bed ... when Blondie started barking, he kicked her out of the room and slammed the door. I tried to get away, but he shoved me face down on the bed, ripped off my panties, and fucked me." I lifted my head. "It was far from an act of love."

"Susan," she said, "he raped you."

16

Dog Fight

Like many victims of sexual assault, I found it difficult to accept the fact that I'd been raped, especially by someone I thought I loved. I couldn't allow the word into my brain, let alone say it out loud, even during my therapy sessions with Beverly. I had to push it out of my brain, like I did with my abortion.

"I know you want to forget about Bobby and what he did to you," Beverly said, "but to normalize and repress rape isn't healthy."

"I just want to move on with my life," I said, grateful my weekly visit had reached the end of its hour.

On my way out the door, Beverly handed me a booklet.

"It's about recovering from rape," she said.

I took the booklet, knowing I'd never read it, and stuffed it under my car seat. Easier to deny the trauma than allow the truth into my psyche. One day, perhaps I'd be able to confront the issue of rape, but not at this time. For now, I needed to focus on getting my belongings out of the apartment.

* * *

At the end of the month, I parked on the street in front of my apartment and waited until the moving truck pulled up in front of me.

"Don't be scared," I told my canine copilot. "I've hired two strong men to help us, and with a bit of luck, the creep won't be home. We'll be in and out in an hour, I promise."

Blondie jumped out of my car and bounded up the stairs. I followed, the brawny movers I'd hired were in tow. When I opened the front door, I saw Bobby passed out on the couch. I figured he must be recovering from another bender.

"Moving day," I said in a fake, cheery voice. The sight of him made me want to run.

He wiped the sleep from his eyes and frowned. "You can't take the bed. Where am I gonna sleep?"

I didn't answer. Instead, I got to work on boxing my things as quickly as possible. The movers took my big items downstairs, leaving me alone with my ex. My hands trembled, but I kept working. The last thing I wanted was for him to sense my fear. I didn't make eye contact and made sure Blondie stayed close by my side.

The movers returned and grabbed more of my stuff. I picked up a box and followed them down the stairs. While we were discussing the best way to pack the van, Blondie growled.

"What is it?" I asked. I followed her gaze and saw Bobby staring over the balcony, his eyes ablaze.

"Bitch!" He threw my favorite pink silk blouse at me.

I watched it dance in the breeze and caught it before it hit the street.

Blondie's hackles were up. She snapped and snarled at Bobby.

"It's okay, girlie," I said as I put her safely in my car.

When I turned around, I saw the movers ducking and dodging while Bobby threw more of my belongings onto the ground.

"This guy's crazy," one of the movers said.

I sighed and shook my head. "No kidding. Let's get this done quickly."

They got to work.

"Calm down," I yelled at Bobby. "Let me get my stuff."

"Here's your stuff," he screamed, his eyes bulging. "Belongs in the gutter, like you!"

I watched Bobby hurl my prized possession—an expensive Nikon camera Dad had bought me. It smashed into pieces about ten feet away, followed by wineglasses and coffee cups.

I shot a glance at the movers and said, "Let's get the hell out of here!"

They didn't need convincing.

I jumped in my car and sped away, leaving the mess in the street. The clean freak who had created it could clean it up.

*   *   *

Angel and I hiked Runyon Canyon the next morning alongside our pack of dogs. I needed to get outside. The canyon, tucked right in the middle of Hollywood, seemed like the perfect place to clear my head. And sure enough, when I stepped onto the East Ridge Trail, my anxiety began to untangle.

"I think I'm an addict too," I said. The morning fog lifted to showcase the sweeping views from Catalina Island to the Santa Monica

Mountains. "I'm addicted to people. In one of my Al-Anon meetings, a woman shared that being around needy people helped her ignore her own issues."

"Makes sense, darling," Angel said. "But don't be too hard on yourself. Bobby fooled us all." She turned to me and stopped for a moment. "Even Presley and Percy liked him. We've all got to learn to set healthy boundaries."

"That's what Beverly talked about. Setting boundaries."

"I'm thrilled you're seeing her, sweetikins."

"Me too. Between therapy sessions and my meetings, I'm learning a lot. It's time I take my own inventory."

"Taking inventory is an excellent way to learn to love yourself. When you take a step back and look inward, you'll be able to accept yourself for who you are—warts and all."

"I hate to look at the things I've done in the past," I said, "but I know you're right. There's even a step in Al-Anon about taking inventory."

We hiked to the top of the canyon and rested on a bench perched high above Los Angeles, where we enjoyed the view of the Pacific Ocean.

"But what about Bobby's inventory?" I asked. "At another meeting, a woman said that when you try to save a drowning man, you run the risk of being pulled under with him. I mean, what if Bobby comes after me? What if he hurts Blondie to get back at me?"

"He won't. Besides, dogs, like children, are resilient," Angel said. "Bobby doesn't know where you're staying, right? And without a car, he'd have a hard time finding you."

I nodded and watched our pups on the trail. They sniffed the native plants and barked at other dogs passing by. I swore I saw a smile on Blondie's face.

"I understand what attracted you to him," Angel said. "I know you wanted to help. But you're not Mother Teresa, and you can't help everyone. You've got to value yourself."

"Kinda like the opposite of the golden rule—treat myself as I would treat others."

"Exactly," she said. "Reminds me of one of my favorite quotes from Carl Jung. He said, 'One does not become enlightened by imagining figures of light, but by making the darkness conscious.' The better you know yourself, the better chance you'll meet a healthy, available man."

"I like that idea. I can't believe I stayed with Bobby for three years. What a waste of time."

"No relationship is a waste of time," Angel said. "Even failure can teach us valuable lessons."

"Jeez, I don't want to go through that shit again. I hope I've learned my lesson."

*　　*　　*

Angel and her family left for the Cape the following week. I appreciated the quiet and used the time to lick my wounds. I read every self-help book I could get my hands on, and, gradually, with the help of my old friend—chocolate ice cream—I began to feel better about my life. There was just one problem—the size of my tummy. It was time to stop hibernating. I needed exercise and to be in the company of human friends.

That was when Ivy, a talented artist and a musician friend I'd met through Bobby, invited Blondie and me to her housewarming party. Her new place was located off Sunset Boulevard above the Rainbow Bar and Grill, affectionately known by trendies as The Rainbow Room. Although she had just moved in, her place already looked like a museum, with original artwork covering the walls. In a word, Ivy was colorful.

Going to a party at her place sounded like fun, as long as I didn't run into my ex. So, before I committed, I asked Ivy if Bobby was going to be there. I sure as hell didn't want to risk seeing him again.

"No," she said. "He's out of town."

With the coast clear,

Portrait of me and Blondie taken by Bobby's artist friend, Ivy Ney.

96

16. Dog Fight

I dressed up in one of Angel's trendy designer outfits, curled my hair, and grabbed Blondie. Together, we headed to the Sunset Strip.

Sure enough, Ivy's party was packed with what I referred to as PIB—people in black—hip, stylish, creative types who dressed entirely in black. While I was too much of a geek to fit in, I relished being close to the *in* crowd.

The best part of Ivy's new place was the window that led to the rooftop. Blondie and I hung out with some PIBs, gabbing and watching the twinkling lights on the strip below. When we headed back inside, I noticed Blondie had her tail between her legs.

"What's wrong, girlie?" I bent down and kissed her head. "You usually love parties."

When I looked up, I saw what was frightening her—Bobby. I had to get out of there as soon as possible. He hadn't seen us, and I wanted to keep it that way. I stayed in the kitchen, secretly watching his every move. When he walked toward the rooftop entrance, I ran out of there like a woman with her hair on fire, Blondie sprinting by my side.

"Come on, girl," I said, my adrenaline pumping.

I glanced over my shoulder and saw Bobby running after us.

"Stop ... stop," he said.

I yelled back at him, "Stay away from us!"

I made it to Sunset Boulevard. So did Bobby. He grabbed my hair and threw me against a brick wall. Blondie barked and growled and lunged at him.

Bobby kicked her back. "You and your stupid fucking dog. You think you're better than me?"

He started pummeling me with his fists, hitting hard. I used my arms to block his blows. But his pounding wouldn't stop. I covered my face with my hands and slowly slid down the wall inch by inch. He punched my hands, arms, ribs, and stomach.

I heard someone yell, "Shut up."

I screamed back, "Call 911!"

The beating stopped, and I heard Blondie whimper. When I looked to see what was wrong, I saw Bobby holding her in the air. She dangled from her leash, her legs flailing in the air.

Bobby glared at me. "You love this damn dog more than me!"

If I didn't do something, she'd choke. I released my inner mama bear, jumped up, made a tight fist, and slugged Bobby in the face. He let go of Blondie and ran his fingers over his bloodied mouth.

I grabbed Blondie's leash and took off up a side street. When we reached my car, we jumped in. I shoved the key into the ignition, threw the car into gear, and got the hell out of there. I didn't look back until I turned off the car. Thankful we'd reached the safe sanctuary of Angel's house.

*   *   *

Beverly handed me a box of Kleenex.

"Bobby beat me up...." I said between sobs. "I can't believe he punched me. I'm scared I'll never get rid of him."

"Drinking and violence can go hand in hand," Beverly said. "Nearly 60 percent of women experience abuse in a relationship. I'm sorry you had to be among that statistic."

"Look," I said, pushing up the sleeves of my sweater. "My arms are black and blue, and my ribs hurt. I can't sleep.... I have flashbacks, even when I'm awake."

"That's normal," she said. "You're experiencing the lingering effects of trauma."

"I'm mortified, and yet, somehow, I still feel like this is my fault. Like the time I made Dad so mad that he hit me."

"Your dad hit you?"

"Twice, actually. I deserved it each time."

"Susan," Beverly said, looking directly into my eyes. "No one deserves physical abuse."

"I did," I countered, staring at Blondie sitting on the floor in front of me. "The first time, Mom found my personal diary and read it. It was full of the crazy things teenagers do. She made me tell Dad every single detail, which made him mad. The second time, I came home, shit-faced drunk. I should've known better."

"Being drunk doesn't give your dad, or anyone, the right to hit you," Beverly said. "People who've been abused can experience post-traumatic stress. They might have difficulty connecting with others or experience low self-esteem. Sound familiar to you?"

I tapped the arm of the love seat and nodded. "Definitely the low self-esteem."

"What I want you to do right now is take steps to protect yourself," Beverly said. She paused and leaned forward. "Did you file a police report about this incident with Bobby?"

"No. When I heard sirens, Blondie and I ran away. I don't know if the police arrived."

"How about a restraining order?"

"I haven't thought about that, either." I slumped back in the love seat. "Do you think I need one? I don't know his current address."

"Let's hope he doesn't have yours." She tucked a strand of hair behind her ear. "If you feel you're in danger, it's important to do whatever's necessary to stay safe. Change your phone number. Plan what to do if he confronts you again."

"I swear, relationships are nothing but pain. I'm afraid to ever date again."

"There are many things we have no control over in life," Beverly said, "like changing someone we care about into the person we want them to be. But taking care of yourself is not on that list. When you care for your own physical, psychological, and spiritual growth, your life will become richer, healthier, and ultimately safer."

"Sign me up," I said.

"Only you have the power to change," Beverly continued. "Self-love is a state of appreciation for one's self. It grows from our actions. The key is to love yourself enough to turn away from something that might seem exciting and instead choose what you need to stay strong and centered, so you can move forward in your life."

"You make it sound so easy."

"It is," she said. "The first step is to protect yourself."

17

All You Need
Is Love—and a Dog

"This summer's flown by," I told Angel over the phone the week before her planned return. "I'm not having much luck in finding an apartment. So far, they're either out of my price range or total dumps."

"No hurry, sweetikins," she replied, "but John's body double, Jason, just told me about a bungalow for rent in Beverly Hills. Interested?"

"Beverly Hills? I can't afford the 90210."

"Jason told me the city's under rent control," she said, a kettle whistling in the background. "The apartment's only $570 a month."

"When can I take a look?"

"Right away," she said. "But before you meet him, I have to warn you, Jason's a poseur."

"What's a poseur?"

"A person who pretends to be someone he's not," she said.

"Well that makes sense. He's John's double; he gets paid to be someone he's not."

"Yeah," Angel said, sipping her tea, "but Jason takes it too far. He even imitates John off camera. I think he takes advantage of his looks."

"Thanks for the heads-up, but don't worry. I'm still in recovery from asshole Bobby. I've sworn off men—at least for now."

"I do worry about you," she said, her voice gentle. "Jason can be manipulative, especially when someone's vulnerable like you are now. I'm certain you'll find him handsome; everyone does. He'll be absolutely charming. Don't fall for him—and don't even consider rebound sex. Jason's trouble."

I nodded. "No dating Jason, but I hope he comes through with the bungalow. Otherwise, I might have to stay with you forever."

* * *

John's double waited for me in front of what I hoped would be my new digs—an older, run-down apartment building near posh Rodeo

17. All You Need Is Love—and a Dog

Drive. There was no mistaking him. He looked like a younger version of John—tall and lanky with the same shy smile. My heart gave a little flutter, and I did the unspeakable—I fluffed my hair. Good thing Angel had warned me.

"Susan?" he asked, taking my hand in his and bringing it to his lips.

I pulled my hand back. "That's me."

"John didn't mention you were so beautiful," he said, purposely bumping his shoulder against mine as if it were a mating call. "A woman like you deserves to live in a palace."

Inwardly, I choked on his rehearsed lines, but outwardly, I kept my cool. "Well, then, hopefully, this bungalow will be fit for royalty like me."

"You're funny too," he said. "That your dog?"

I pointed to Blondie. "You mean this gorgeous girl sitting obediently by my side? Yeah, she's mine. Her name's Blondie. I rescued her from the pound."

"She's a beauty, too," Jason said.

He moved a little too close, and his warm breath brushed my cheek. I took another step back, but his fresh, citrusy scent had already given me goose bumps.

"I used to have a Labrador," he said. "Went with me everywhere."

God help me, he's a dog lover! Maybe he's not that bad. Or is this part of his act?

He went on, "Lost him to cancer a couple years ago."

Did he brush a tear away? I pulled myself together. Didn't matter if he was really into me or just pretending in order to work his way into my pants. I'd come protected. I wore an imaginary coat of armor—an idea that struck me after a recent therapy session—a way to guard myself. A coat of armor in the form of a Catwoman suit had seemed perfect, impossible to penetrate. Hopefully....

"Not sure the landlord allows dogs."

"I'm happy to leave an extra pet deposit," I said.

"But you haven't seen the place yet." He gestured toward the bungalow. "Might be too small. Follow me. It's in the back, above a garage."

Casanova gave me a wink, grabbed my hand, and guided me across the front lawn. He definitely seemed more determined to hook up than show me the apartment. I needed a home, not a boyfriend. But I didn't want to alienate him, not when he held the key to my possible future home. I remembered my armor.

"Do you live in the building?" I asked, following him up the stairs.

"No," he answered. "I live up the street. I'm friends with the owner.

Already put in a good word for you. I'd love to show you around town. The best restaurants, clubs, bars are within walking distance. You'll like it here."

While Jason flirted his ass off, Blondie ran ahead and stopped at the front door, no doubt her psychic canine instinct guiding her.

"I'm sure we will. Won't we, girl?"

"I've got a truck, and I would be happy to help you move. I'm pretty good at hanging artwork too."

I was surprised he hadn't invited me to see his etchings.

He continued, "Or maybe you'd allow me to take you out for a drink tonight?"

"Ah," I said, "let's see if I get the apartment first."

No way would I hook up with Jason. He acted too eager, stiff, rehearsed. Been there, done that. Jason might look like John, but he sure as hell lacked his humble qualities. *Wait until Beverly hears about my progress.*

Jason opened the front door to reveal a quaint space. Milky-white walls trimmed with fancy crown molding. The morning sun filtered through oversize windows and gave the place a bright ambiance. A small table with two chairs would fit perfectly in the kitchen. I imagined my bed taking up most of the tiny bedroom, but the enormous built-in closet would help me keep everything organized.

"Here's the best part," Jason said. "The bathroom. All original deco tile."

He posed against the sink like a Calvin Klein model, but he was right about the pink-tiled bathroom. It clinched the deal for me.

"I love it," I said. "You do, too, don't you, girl?"

Blondie looked up at me and wagged her tail.

"When can we move in?" I pulled out my checkbook.

"Hold on," he said, moving closer. "You need to fill out an application form, and I need to tell you the owner's already taken a ton."

"Darn!" I said. "I really need this place."

Jason hit me with another wink. "Let's see what I can do."

* * *

Tuned out, Jason didn't let me down. I got the bungalow and moved in right after Angel and her family returned from the Cape. After I finished unpacking, Blondie and I sat on our new, secondhand couch. I looked around and beamed. My furniture fit perfectly, and I hoped my life would fall into place just as easily. With her head in my lap, my canine savior gazed up at me with her amber puppy-dog eyes.

17. All You Need Is Love—and a Dog

"You don't have to be scared anymore." I stroked her golden coat. "Bobby's gone ... for good. I'm so sorry I didn't protect you better. Or myself. Because of you, I came to my senses. By saving you, I rescued myself."

I hadn't felt that good in a long, long time.

I gazed at my vision board hanging on the wall before me, the one I'd made with Angel pre–Bobby. "I promise I'll never date anyone who drinks like that."

Blondie placed her paw on my arm as if she understood and then gave me her seal of approval with a big, wet kiss.

* * *

During my next session with Beverly, I broached the subject of dating. In the back of my mind, I still craved companionship from a two-legged mortal.

"I haven't met anyone who'd be considered marriage material," I said. "All the men I meet seem damaged in one way or another."

"Everyone's damaged," Beverly said. "It's impossible not to be. There's an old saying: *a knight in shining armor hasn't yet seen battle.* If you're not scuffed up, scratched up, and torn up, you haven't lived your life."

"I don't need a knight." I ran my hand through my hair. "If I imagine myself wearing a suit of armor—Catwoman-style with a whip—I feel strong and protected without a man."

"That's an interesting idea," she said, crossing her legs, "to feel confident and protected. When you started working with me, you had forgotten about protecting yourself, remember? You jumped into relationships before considering the personal consequences that came with the package. I see real progress."

"That's true, but I still need to learn how to date."

"You've acknowledged how and why you allowed your past boyfriend to control your emotions and behavior and how you can't change anyone."

"And I've learned the hard way to value my safety," I said.

Beverly nodded. "Absolutely! Plus, you've witnessed firsthand how being with the wrong man can negatively affect your health and well-being. Always remember, you have a choice when it comes to your life."

"What choice do I have when it comes to meeting Mr. Right? Seems like most men are either in a committed relationship or complete wackos." I crossed my arms.

Beverly smiled. "You could meet Mr. Right anywhere. You've worked hard to develop the tools to protect yourself when it comes to dating. Consider places where a healthy, balanced man might spend his time."

"My parents met at church. They're always pestering me to join one, but I'm not so sure I want to take dating advice from them."

"Wait a minute." Beverly tapped a finger on her lips. "Church is a good place to meet a man. He'd most likely be grounded. He'd be attending church for spiritual growth, to socialize with other members of the community, to make business contacts, develop friends. There's really no downside."

"I'd welcome a spiritually inclined man." I looked down at Blondie for agreement. "But church?"

"Why not? These days, there are countless ways to meet a man."

I must not have looked convinced.

Beverly continued, "How about Great Expectations?"

"Isn't that video dating?" I asked.

"What's wrong with that?"

"Those places are for losers, people who can't get a date."

She smoothed her skirt. "I actually know a couple who met through Great Expectations. They're perfect for each other."

"There's got to be another way," I said, shaking my head.

"Susan, you can date any way you want. This is your life, remember?"

I let out a heavy sigh. *Kill me now.*

18

Love Quest, Doggie Style

I took Blondie with me to shoot my video at Great Expectations. The studio was nothing fancy. It consisted of a white backdrop, a single chair facing a video camera, and a bunch of miscellaneous crap in a corner. Rod, the cameraman, resembled a Pekingese on a bad hair day. But he looked the part of a video dating concierge with his spiky hair and white button-down dress shirt.

"Your dog in this too?" Rod asked, scratching his head. "That's a first."

I nodded. "Blondie goes everywhere with me."

She looked adorable. I'd clipped pink bows behind her ears.

He motioned for me to sit on a folding chair next to a fake palm tree.

"Can I get an extra chair for my dog?" I asked.

Rod headed to the pile of crap in the corner and pulled out a pint-sized table and placed it next to me. Blondie jumped up and sat like Gloria Swanson in the film *Sunset Boulevard*, waiting for her close-up. I held the script I'd written in my hand and wondered what the hell I was doing here.

"And action," Rod said, pointing to me like he was directing *Gone with the Wind*.

After a few seconds of awkward silence, I stared into the camera lens and said, "I'm S-S-Susan, and this is my dog, Blondie." I stroked her head. "I work in public relations. I'm as comfortable in blue jeans as I am in a cocktail dress. Blondie and I enjoy long walks on the beach." I glanced at my notes and wondered why the hell I had written that last sentence. Blondie and I rarely took long walks on the beach. "A sense of humor is important to me, but a love of animals is critical."

As if on cue, Blondie barked. Rod jumped.

I continued, "I'd like to have a family of my own one day with a loving husband. Oh, and I'm looking for someone with a good job and a steady income. Someone who wants to share their life with me and my precious pup."

I leaned over and gave Blondie a kiss on her nose. The table rocked, Blondie jumped off, causing it to crash against the wall.

I looked at Rod.

"That's a wrap," he said.

Rod directed me and Blondie to a viewing room where I looked through videos of available men. I sat in front of a monitor while Blondie made herself comfortable at my feet. I hit play with the excitement of a first grader about to watch the Cookie Monster.

A man with a missing front tooth, wearing a wrinkled button-down shirt, came into focus. "I'm looking for a woman who takes great pride in her appearance."

"Poor guy," I said to Blondie. "He obviously doesn't own a mirror."

Next in line, a conservative-looking man in a business suit, complete with a striped tie and button-down vest, wearing a Donny Osmond smile, stared at me. He reminded me of James, the preppy boy I'd let slip away in favor of Bobby.

"I like to wrap myself in Scotch tape and roll around the floor," he said. "I have fun and clean my carpet at the same time."

"Fun … with Scotch tape?"

Blondie lifted her head and nudged my leg.

Mr. Conservative ran his tongue over his lips.

"Things might get a bit sticky around this lunatic, hey, girlie?" I hit fast-forward and leaned closer to the monitor when Alex—a handsome, well-spoken anesthesiologist—introduced himself.

I reached down and patted Blondie. "Now we're talking."

*   *   *

Alex and I decided to meet for sushi. I scanned the restaurant and saw him sitting at the counter. His video hadn't lied; he was handsome.

"Alex?" I asked, putting on my best sexy Sharon Stone voice.

"Susan," he said. "Are you ready for the best sushi you've ever had?" He stood and pulled out the chair next to him.

It seemed that God had put his energy into Alex's Robert Redford good looks and not in his height. He stood on his tiptoes to kiss me Euro-style and then grabbed my biceps.

"Sturdy stock," he said.

"Strong hands," I replied. "Are you shopping for livestock?"

My words went over his head.

He raised an eyebrow. "Do you exercise?"

"I power-walk with my dog, Blondie," I lied. He didn't have to know that by power-walk, I meant powering through a bar of chocolate while Blondie ran around the dog park.

"You need to do more than that," he said, rolling up his sleeves and flexing his biceps. "Think about your heart."

"You're right," I said as his face morphed into an English bulldog.

"After dinner, why don't you ride my bike, and I'll jog alongside you?" he said. "It'll be fun."

Fun, my ass!

After dinner, I followed Alex's Mercedes convertible to a luxury high-rise on Wilshire Boulevard. A concierge waited out front with a bicycle by his side. Alex palmed him a few dollars, took the bike, and wheeled it over to me.

"Ready for an adventure?" he asked.

"I guess so." I hoisted up my skirt and eased my butt onto the seat, noting that Alex's bike probably cost more than my car.

"Just a sec," he said, switching out his loafers for a pair of jogging shoes the concierge had handed him.

Alex took off like a greyhound. He didn't jog; he ran. Fast! I couldn't keep up, let alone hold a conversation. A Karmann Ghia blew through a yellow light. I glared at the driver, a handsome young male who waved at me as he drove past. My heart went aflutter, and the bike wobbled. I fought to keep my balance and from getting my high heels caught in the pedals.

A Celica cut in front of me and stopped short. I hit the brakes and managed to stop myself from flying over the handlebars.

Alex was barely a dot in the distance.

"Fuck this shit!" I turned the bike around and headed back to his building.

The concierge seemed surprised to see me back so soon, but asked no questions. I handed him the bike and made a quick getaway in my car.

* * *

I brought Blondie along for my next date, just in case the guy suggested I hop on his horse. Besides, having her with me took the pressure off and gave me confidence.

Mr. Armani Pants showed up, looking like a *GQ* model; I liked what I saw. But I knew this date was doomed when I noticed the fur left in his hand after he gave Blondie a quick pat.

"Does she shed like that all the time?" he asked.

Next!

I'm Not Single, I Have a Dog

Mike looked like a giant teddy bear. Not my usual type, but that was the plan, right? He didn't mention Blondie's presence when we showed up together to join him on the restaurant patio.

"My wife and I separated several months ago," he said. "We split shortly after the birth of our daughter. She'll be twelve months old next month." He pulled a picture of a baby out of his wallet that looked to me like a geriatric pug. "She's so cute, look."

"Adorable," I said, chugging my wine. "I love babies," I added. "How can you stand being away from her? I can't stomach leaving my dog at home, and we're not even the same species." I took a look at Blondie under the table.

"That's what kills me," Mike said, sweat beading on his forehead. "I saw my baby girl the moment she took her first breath."

"I'd think having a baby would bring a couple closer together. But what do I know?"

Mike excused himself to use the men's room. I sat there for about ten minutes, downing my wine and eating all the bread in the basket. Finally, he returned.

"I thought you'd gotten lost," I said.

"Not at all. In fact, I've been found, thanks to you. I called my wife, and we've decided to work things out. We're getting back together. I get to tuck my baby girl into bed tonight." He threw a twenty-dollar bill on the table. "This should cover the wine."

I watched as he strode out of the restaurant and into the distance. *Next!*

Mr. New Age, a big-time movie producer, confessed on our first date that he hadn't had sex in ten years. He'd taken a vow of chastity in order to be closer to God. *Why in the hell had he signed up for Great Expectations?*

"Something awoke inside me when I saw you," he said.

"Yeah," I muttered under my breath, "your penis."

I finally mastered the art of the first date like my therapist had suggested. But I found Great Expectations exhausting, and after a couple of months, I canceled my membership.

However, I wasn't ready to give up on my dream of finding a husband. So I found a group called Young Executive Singles, or YES. It seemed like a good place to meet a career man. At least I'd be able to network.

The Century City restaurant was packed with singles in their twenties and thirties looking for love. My nerves had kept me from eating the entire day, but I was determined to make the best of the opportunity, so I plastered a smile on my face to make my entrance.

Once inside, I took a deep breath and headed to the bar. A drink would settle my nerves. I felt a little unsteady. Maybe I should've eaten something. My head started to spin. Then everything went black.

I fainted right there in the middle of everything. I woke, splayed out on the floor, my skirt hiked up, panties on display, with a strange group of networkers surrounding me.

I wanted to cry, wanted to die right there.

Time to face the facts. My only choice left was church.

19

Father, Son and Holy Dog

Angel was a longtime member of All Saints' Episcopal Church in Beverly Hills. I'd gone with her family to celebrate Easter and Christmas but never attended a regular Sunday service.

"I had that dream again last night," Angel told me on the way to her church. "You know, the one where you meet your handsome prince."

"Really?" I stared out the car window, hoping her dream was an omen that I'd meet someone at church.

"Yes, darling," she said. "Just like in the movies. The two of you declare your love for each other in my backyard."

We entered the church parking lot and found a spot right in the front. Another good omen. Angel took my hand, and we headed inside.

The morning light streamed through massive stained-glass windows and added a warm glow to the nave. Ornate chandeliers hung from the ceiling, and the scent of incense made me hopeful this would work.

When the service started, I noticed a man sitting on his own a few rows in front of us. His shoulder-length brown hair hit the top of a sharp navy-blue sports coat. Normally, I steered clear of guys with long hair, but there was something about this man that made me curious.

"I see what you're looking at," Angel said.

I felt a rush of heat on my face.

"Darling, you've got to meet him," she whispered.

After the service, Angel tugged at my dress, waiting for the stranger to walk by. One look at his blue eyes, and I was a goner. Angel pushed me forward, so I walked out of the sanctuary beside him.

Once outside, I turned to face him, but my mind went blank.

"Oh, hi," he said, holding out his hand. "I'm Jack."

The minute our skin touched, I felt a tingle up my arm, all the way to my heart and then a little further south.

19. *Father, Son and Holy Dog*

When I didn't say anything, Angel nudged me. That was when I realized I still had a tight grip on this man's hand and had gone mute.

"Hi, Jack. I'm Angel." She put her arm around me. "This is my single friend Susan. Are you single?"

"Angel! You're making me look desperate." I looked at Jack and said, "I'm not desperate, I swear!" I dropped his hand, but the tingle remained.

"What brings you to All Saints'?" Angel asked.

"A friend of mine told me about this place," he said. "I especially liked the acoustics."

"You look familiar, Jack," Angel said. "Have we met before?"

"I don't think so," he said, "but I get that a lot."

"Are you an actor?" I asked. The tingle turned into a pulsing throb between my legs.

"No, I'm a musician."

God help me.

* * *

From that day on, I became a weekly regular at All Saints.' With one eye on my spiritual well-being, the other searched the pews for Jack. One day, I noticed him sitting alone. His eyes closed, he seemed tranquil and lost in the music drifting through the church.

I walked over to him. When he opened his eyes and looked up at me, that tingle returned.

"Do you want to join me?" He slid over to allow me to sit beside him.

"This music is gorgeous," I said.

"It's a Bach's 'Brandenburg' Concerto," he said. "Are you familiar with Bach?"

"Sure, I know his name. I'm just not familiar with the names of his pieces."

The music faded, replaced by the voices of the choir as they walked up the aisle.

Throughout the service, I had a hard time keeping my mind on the present. Every time I glanced at Jack, my heart fluttered.

On our way outside to fellowship, Jack asked, "Wanna join me for lunch?"

"Sure," I said a little too quickly, "as long as we go somewhere dog-friendly."

"You have a dog?"

"Sure do," I said. "A pound mutt. Her name's Blondie."

"After the band?"

111

"Exactly. She's my girl."

"How about we meet at Café des Artistes?"

"My favorite. It's a date—I mean, I'll see you there."

* * *

When Blondie and I entered the restaurant patio, the sweet scent of roses filled the air. I looked around, and when I didn't see Jack, I grabbed a table, and Blondie settled on the ground next to me.

"Sorry I'm late," Jack said. "Had to put gas in my car." He bent down to Blondie. "What a cool-looking dog. You look like a white wolf." He scratched under her chin. "Ahh, here's your sweet spot."

She bent her head back in ecstasy, scratching his hand with her back leg.

"Congratulations," I announced. "You passed the Blondie test."

"The what?"

"You must be a good person," I said. "She sniffs out the bad ones for me."

He locked eyes with Blondie. "You're not just a pretty face, are you, girl? You're a prophet."

His leg bounced to the beat of the background music.

"Want to split a pizza?" he asked.

"Sounds good." I looked at the waiter. "Can we get separate checks?" I turned my focus back to Jack. "So tell me about your music. What do you play? Or do you sing?"

Right: Photograph strip of me and Blondie (photographs by Susanne Hayek).

112

"I play bass," he said, "and write a bit. I've had my share of luck in the music biz. MCA Records signed my band a few years back."

"You don't seem like a typical musician. The ones I've met aren't very religious. They're into drugs and alcohol, not God."

"Not me," he said. "I've never been one to drink much, and I hate drugs. But I'm not into religion either. I grew up Catholic, but now, I consider myself more spiritual than anything else."

"Are you a recovering Catholic?" I'd heard that term used in my Al-Anon meetings.

"Yes, I guess I am."

"I love the bass guitar." I eyed his kissable lips. "It's the heartbeat of any band. You must be talented to have been signed."

"I don't know about that." He added cream to his coffee. "But all I've ever wanted to do is play in a band."

"So nice to meet someone who's doing what they love," I said.

"Not quite," he said. "Right now, I make ends meet by working at the Youth Authority. I'm a drug and HIV counselor."

"Are you sober yourself? I mean are you a member of AA?"

"No, but I've been to many meetings. It's a long story."

"I'd love to hear it someday."

Lunch arrived, causing Blondie to wake up from her afternoon nap. She hoped one of us would give her a bite—or two—of our pizza.

"Not for you," I told her and then looked at Jack and those dreamy blue eyes of his. "How did you end up working in the Youth Authority?"

"Good question." He fidgeted in his seat. "Originally, I wanted to work as a therapist and help other musicians who were using. But after my last record deal went nowhere, I headed back to college, graduated from UCLA in psychology, and kind of fell into this job."

"That's honorable of you," I said. "People who help children are real heroes."

"These kids are incarcerated for a reason. It's a good day when I leave there alive."

"Come on. It can't be that bad."

"I just have to watch my back, that's all."

"Where'd you grow up?" I dabbed my mouth with a napkin, hoping I didn't have grease dripping down my chin from the pizza.

"Panorama City."

"I'm from the Valley too." I wanted to grab his face and kiss him on the mouth right there. Such a catch and so much in common.

"What are you doing after lunch?" he asked, inhaling his pizza.

"I planned to take Blondie on a hike."

"Wanna take her to the beach instead? I know about a dog-friendly stretch in Malibu. Should be a magical sunset."

* * *

I pulled up behind Jack's BMW on PCH, leashed Blondie, and walked onto the sand to meet Jack. When I unleashed her, Blondie took off, running in happy puppy circles.

Jack was right. The sky lit up in bright pinks, yellows, and a hint of orange, and a full moon peeked over the horizon.

"You studied psychology," I said. "Do you consider yourself a Freudian or a Jungian?"

"I'm more of a Jungian," Jack said. "I like his ideas about striving for wholeness, not perfection. But right now, I'm reading Joseph Campbell. You heard of him?"

"No, never."

"Campbell says you should follow your bliss."

"Follow your bliss," I said. "I like that."

"I meditate every day ... have been into transcendental meditation for years now."

"My brother's into TM," I said. "I've wanted to learn since I heard about The Beatles and their famous guru."

"You mean Maharishi Mahesh Yogi? My teacher's nothing like him. Why don't you come with me sometime and see for yourself?"

20

Fashion Faux Paws

"Allow your thoughts to flow like a stream," Jack's guru, Charlie, said. "One thought after the other. Watch them float away."

A small gray-haired man, Jack's guru looked more like Alex Trebek than a teacher in transcendental meditation.

"TM helps you break through your restful state of mind beyond thoughts," he said like it was the answer to a *Jeopardy!* question.

It didn't matter what he looked like. I liked Charlie immediately. So did the fifty-plus people gathered in a simple meeting room in Santa Monica that evening. The stark white room was filled with folding chairs facing a podium where Charlie led the meditation. I couldn't wait to get started.

"Practicing TM helps you master the stress. If you're looking for energy, creativity, and awareness, you've come to the right place."

"I want that," I whispered to Jack.

My mind seemed calm, but there was a giant barrier. My heart raced—the result of sitting so close to Jack. *How could I conquer my restless thoughts when our legs touched?* I had to admit, the rush felt good.

"Charlie's so normal," I whispered. "I expected a turban-wearing holy man with a long beard."

"That's why I like him," Jack said. "He's so normal that he could be your next-door neighbor. For your mantra, just think of a word that'll make you feel happy."

"What's a mantra?"

Jack raised his eyebrows and said, "Some call it a tool of the mind; others say it's an instrument of thought. Whatever you call it, just pick a word that brings you joy and focus on it during the meditation."

"Do you have a mantra?" I asked.

"Yep," he answered, "but I can't tell you. I can't tell anyone."

I decided to make the word *Blondie* my mantra. That dog made me so happy. Once I began thinking of her, I relaxed. The lights dimmed, and it seemed everyone in the room took a deep breath in unison.

I'm Not Single, I Have a Dog

I closed my eyes and sat back, relaxed in my chair. Maybe TM held the secret for me. Or maybe Jack did. I let those thoughts float downstream, and before I knew it, twenty minutes had flown by.

Jack stroked my shoulder to bring me back to reality. "We're done. You can stop meditating now."

I opened my eyes, my mind fuzzy. "I didn't levitate or anything, but still, I can't believe how good I feel. Like I'm connected to everything. Why doesn't everyone meditate?"

Jack smiled. "I'd hoped you'd get it."

It didn't take long for the fluttering in my stomach to return. Something about Jack made me want to get closer to him. But I worried about letting my guard down. The thought of opening up to another musician scared the hell out of me.

*   *   *

I met Angel for coffee later that week at a little dog-friendly place on Melrose. We sat on the patio, and Blondie and Hobson lay at our feet, squished as close together as possible.

"I haven't heard from Jack in two days."

"Darling, two days is nothing," she said, sipping her coffee.

"Look at our dogs; they're totally in love." I patted the top of Blondie's head, but she didn't move an inch from her boyfriend. "Why can't humans be more like that? We're so complicated. Dogs aren't."

Angel looked at the happy canine couple. "I had a feeling about you and Jack the moment we met him at church. Consider developing your friendship first … get to know him before you get physical."

"That's what Beverly says."

"Listen to her," Angel said. "She's a smart lady. I fell hard when I first met John, but he insisted we establish a friendship first. Now, I'm so happy he did. Think about it. As friends, you're already comfortable with each other by the time you take the next step. I believe in order for a relationship to be successful, there must be a balance between liking and desiring."

"That makes sense."

"There's really no downside to starting as friends," Angel added.

"So what's the key to making a relationship work?"

"That's a good question. I think the key is having a sense of humor. Laughing together has helped John and me through tough times and brought us closer."

"Friendship and a sense of humor. I got it."

*   *   *

20. Fashion Faux Paws

With Angel's sage advice in mind, I invited Jack to an exclusive reception for French fashion designer Thierry Mugler. Turned out Mugler was Jack's favorite designer. He even owned a suit made by the man known as the Prophet of Futurism.

Jack's interest in Mugler didn't surprise me. He was a fashionista with his combat boots and chain wallet. But I couldn't imagine him in one of Mugler's modernistic designs. To me, they screamed George Jetson cartoon.

We arrived at the designer's exclusive boutique on Rodeo Drive. Beautiful female and male models sashayed around the room in Mugler's trademark designs—dresses with oversize shoulders and men's suits featuring crazy, slick lines.

Jack acted like Blondie when she smelled turkey. "Mugler never uses prints," he said. "He sticks with solid colors. Look at how he puts it all together. Nobody does it like him."

I really didn't get it but nodded anyway. "How could you sit in that hula hoop dress? And check out that guy's suit. I can't imagine sitting opposite him in a board room meeting, let alone next to him. That flame-like collar looks like it could do some serious damage."

"I know," Jack said. "Isn't it amazing?"

I spotted the handsome designer. He looked totally down to earth in a simple white T-shirt and jeans, such a juxtaposition to his designer clothing line. People loved it, and they queued up, waiting for their turn to shake his hand.

"Want to meet him?" I asked.

"No," Jack said. "I don't want to look like a groupie." He handed me a glass of champagne. "It's Cristal."

"Only the best for us," I said. "Cheers."

We checked out all the outrageously expensive clothes on the racks.

I pulled out a plain white blouse and said, "Now, this is more my style."

"You should try it on," Jack said. "It'd look great on you."

"You think so?" I checked the price tag. "Not as expensive as I thought. Only two hundred fifty dollars. This fabric is so … luxurious."

"You should get it," he said. "I spent a fortune on my Mugler suit."

I looked closer at the price tag. "Oops, it's twenty-five hundred. For a white cotton blouse?"

We laughed.

By the end of the night, I noticed Jack staring at me. His blue eyes reflected an intensity that hadn't been there before. My heart fluttered.

"You're giving me that look." I pointed a finger at him.

"What look?"

"You know, *that* look." I couldn't say anything more. Standing next to him made me tongue-tied.

"I have no idea what you're talking about." He kissed my lips. "Thank you so much for inviting me tonight. I can't remember the last time I had this much fun."

He took my hand in his and rubbed his thumb back and forth along my palm. His skin felt soft. The hairs on the back of my neck rose.

"I need another drink," I said.

We headed toward the bar, hand in hand, like lovers. He ordered each of us a glass of champagne.

"Wait," he said. "Let's toast."

"Okay," I said, raising my glass. "To what?"

"To 'that look' and many others to come."

"Cheers," I said, keeping myself from jumping up and down right there in the high-end designer boutique.

After we tapped glasses, he took mine and placed it alongside his on a table. With "that look," Jack so gently put his arms around me. He held me close and ran a hand up and down my back. I realized we were moving out of the friend zone. And I stopped resisting.

Jack and I went back to my place and celebrated more than the fashion show; we celebrated the beginning of our romance.

21

In Dog I Trust.
In Myself, Not So Much

I almost canceled my next session with Beverly. I didn't want to admit that Jack and I had passed the boundary of friendship already. But I put my big-girl panties on and showed up.

"I did it again," I said. "I had sex too soon. I'm doomed when it comes to relationships."

"That's not true," Beverly said. "You got to know him a little before you jumped into bed. There's still time to pull back and allow the relationship to blossom."

"Jack and I talked about the importance of taking it slow," I said. "Neither of us wants to crash and burn."

"Then slow down, take your time. Learn more about each other, examine what you have in common."

"Great idea," I said. "But I haven't heard from him since he slept over. It's been five days."

"What do you know about him?"

"He was engaged but didn't tie the knot. They were together for fifteen years. Jack, the rock-and-roll star, and Charlotte, the model."

"What happened? Why didn't they get married?"

"That's a good question," I said, twirling my hair. "I don't know. They lived in Europe together, traveled, planned on starting a family someday."

"You need to explore why it didn't work out." She looked up from her notepad. "A fifteen-year relationship is substantial."

"I know he's dated other women since. I also know he's still friends with Charlotte."

"Well, that's a good sign," Beverly said. "If they're still friends, at least he ended a longterm relationship in an adult way. Tell me what you like about him."

"Everything."

She paused and then said, "Be more specific."

I'm Not Single, I Have a Dog

"He makes me calm. We laugh. He listens to me, and I feel content and loved when I'm with him. And he's got a job! A real job."

"Okay, that's a good start. Now, we have to wait and see how he handles pressure, if he's stable and reliable."

I had no idea crisis would strike so soon.

* * *

That evening, the entire city of Los Angeles went on lockdown after the acquittal of four police officers who had used excessive force in the videotaped beating of Rodney King. Following the verdict, thousands of people rioted for six solid days.

I watched the news with my neighbors, huddled together to witness what was supposed to be a peaceful, civil protest but quickly escalated into riots, lootings, and arson. The whole chaotic scene was hard to watch but impossible to turn away from.

The news actually showed people setting fires and looting local businesses. Store owners in Koreatown carried their weapons to protect their property. When I saw a light-skinned motorist get pulled out of his truck and beaten, my mind flashed to Jack. I'd never been to his place, but I knew he lived in an area called the Miracle Mile District, which was near the violence, so I ran home to call him.

"Are you okay?" I asked.

"I'm surrounded by smoke," he said and then coughed. "One of the fires is right around the corner."

"The Beverly Hills cops shut everything down here," I told him. "They didn't allow any protesters to enter the city. We're safe, but it's eerily quiet."

"It's anything but quiet here," Jack said.

I heard sirens in the background.

"Why don't you come over? We can ride this out together."

* * *

I hugged Jack tight the moment he arrived, my television blaring in the background. "I'm so glad you came. But I need to know, why didn't you call me after we slept together?" I couldn't help but blurt out my original concern.

"It's a long story," Jack said. "Basically, I didn't want to act too eager. You know, the rules of dating."

"Let's throw out those rules and create our own," I said and then leaned in for a kiss.

So much for taking it slow.

120

21. In Dog I Trust. In Myself, Not So Much

* * *

One clear, starry night, Jack and I walked hand in hand down Melrose on our way to dinner. He had a favorite Italian place he wanted to share with me. Out of nowhere, he stopped in his tracks, grabbed me right there on the sidewalk, and kissed me with an intensity I'd never experienced.

"Thank God," he said, looking up to the heavens. "I'm so grateful I found you."

He stared at me with those blue eyes, and I melted. His sweet gesture filled my heart. I wanted to believe Jack saw me, the real me, and loved me anyway.

But in time, I found that was far from the truth. Jack, the fashionista, had a lot to say about my outward appearance. He didn't like it.

"Your wardrobe needs help," he informed me. "You don't even have the basics, and your hair—we'll need to do something about that."

I interpreted his interest in my wardrobe and hairstyle as a sign of love. I tried to convince myself that I liked his attention. It never occurred to me that he was trying to change me, just like I'd tried to change the other men in my life. Besides, what woman wouldn't want to be with a man who liked to shop?

"I can't believe you don't have a little black dress," he said while we shopped at the Beverly Center. "Every woman needs a little black dress as her staple."

"I guess I'll have to get one right away."

"Your haircut is so dated too," Jack said. "I'll take you to my stylist; she'll fix you."

I'd never had a man offer negative comments about my style, but what the hell? His hairdresser gave me a new look that emphasized my natural wavy hair. I'd spent years blow-drying it straight, so I loved the wash-and-wear idea, but it turned out to be a little more complicated than that.

First, I had to buy a certain shampoo. Next, a new blow dryer. Not just any blow dryer. Jack's hairdresser convinced me to purchase a fancy ceramic model that cost me almost three hundred dollars. Third, a special diffuser, not the one that came with the blow dryer. Plus finishing hair mousse, gel, and serum that also cost a fortune.

It took me a good hour to get my wash-and-ready naturally wavy hair to look like it had the day I left the salon.

* * *

My relationship with Jack heated up quickly. I liked how my future looked. Still, I'd kept our relationship a secret from Mom and Dad. But now that Jack and I were actively looking for a place to live together, I had to fess up.

"I met someone at church," I told Mom over the phone. "His name is Jack. He works at the Youth Authority, helping kids in crisis."

"See?" Mom said. "You should've listened to us a long time ago. You wouldn't have wasted so much time with those losers."

I wanted to throw the phone against the wall.

"I can't wait to meet this Jack," she said.

Dad joined the call. "What's this about a fine church-going man? That's all your mother and I have ever wanted for you. Let's celebrate. We'll take you to dinner."

"I can't wait for you to meet Jack. You'll love him!"

I truly wanted Mom and Dad to like Jack, but I knew in my heart that he was far from the conservative, religious man they hoped I'd marry.

Jack and I arrived early at the swanky Beverly Hills restaurant, and I immediately saw Mom and Dad waiting in the foyer. Mom resembled a cupcake. She sported a tacky-looking bright-pink straw hat that clashed with her matronly red-green-and-purple-sprinkled dress. *What would Jack think of her?*

"Hello, Jack," Dad said as we entered. "It's nice to meet the man of my daughter's dreams."

The two men in my life shook hands.

"Nice to meet you too, Mr. Hartzler." Jack turned to Mom. "That's a lovely dress you're wearing. I can see where Susan inherited her taste in clothes."

I died inside, but Jack winked at me and made it all better.

Mom eyed my little black dress.

"Come on, Mom," I said, cutting her off before she let loose with some remark about me looking like a cheap hooker. I nudged her elbow and guided her to the hostess stand. "You'll love the food here; it's delicious."

"I hope it's as good as Carrows," she mumbled. "They're hard to beat, you know."

Jack and Dad were talking music, their favorite subject.

I took the opportunity to pull Mom aside and asked, "What do you think?"

She nodded with that grin on her face that I knew was totally fake. I could never count on believing most of what she said. Mom lied to people all the time, telling them what she thought they wanted to hear, only to admit her true feelings to me later. That behavior had sure confused me as a kid. I'd been taught never to lie.

Dad put his arm around me and said, "If you two lovebirds get married right away, Susan could be pregnant by her next birthday."

"Dad...."

"We could go to the courthouse right now," he said, and he really meant it. Sometimes, it seemed that Dad wanted me to be married more than I did.

"Sorry to disappoint you, but we're not ready to get married right now." I grabbed Jack's hand. "But we did have something to tell you."

"Really?" Mom said, a look of concern erasing her phony smile.

"Jack and I are looking for a place to move into ... together."

"Now, Susan," Mom scolded me right there at the table, speaking loud enough for the entire restaurant to hear. "How many times have I warned you? Why would a man buy the cow when you he could drink the milk for free?"

"Come on, Margaret," Dad said. "I trust Suzie's judgment. Besides, he seems like a nice enough man."

"Better than the last one." Mom plastered on that fake smile again. "I don't want to see her get hurt again, that's all."

"My intentions are honorary, Mrs. Hartzler," Jack chimed in. "I'm in love with your daughter."

I squeezed his hand and said, "And I love you too."

Dad brushed his hands together and said, "Get busy, you two. I want some grandchildren."

"Slow down, Dad." I loved that Dad approved of Jack. Then again, he really liked my Quaalude-addicted college boyfriend.

The evening went much better than I'd expected. Everyone seemed to get along. Dad obviously liked Jack; the two of them discussed music all night.

After dinner, I headed to the ladies' room with Mom. I couldn't wait to hear what she thought.

"Thanks for dinner, Mom," I said as the restroom door closed behind us.

"That Jack, he's going to be completely bald."

22

No Fleabag, Please

Jack and I found a perfect dog-friendly apartment not far from his place in the Miracle Mile District. The new high-rise building came with a dishwasher, fireplace, central air, floor-to-ceiling windows, and a roof-top pool. I was in heaven, surrounded by such luxury. We happily paid the deposit and signed a one-year lease. As much as I liked the cheap rent of my Beverly Hills apartment, I couldn't wait to move in with Jack and start our lives together. I envisioned this change in our relationship as the first step toward marriage and the family I craved.

Two days before our big move, while Jack and I were walking Blondie, I noticed he seemed a little distant.

"Are you okay?" I asked.

"I'm not sure about this move," he said. "I forgot to mention, I'm allergic to fleas."

"Come on. You know Blondie doesn't have fleas. I treat her every month." I stopped walking and turned to him. "We signed a lease, for God's sake."

"I know," he said, "but dogs are dirty."

"What? I get her groomed every month. Besides, you've never complained before, even when she crawls into bed."

"Well, she barks a lot."

"She's a dog, and no, she doesn't bark too much," I said. "Why on earth are you bringing all this up now? We had this conversation months ago. Remember? Besides, everything's arranged and boxed up. It's too late to turn back now."

He draped an arm around my shoulders. "You're right." He pulled me in for a kiss. "It's ridiculous that we're both paying rent when we're together all the time."

I placed a hand on his chest, "Are you sure?"

"Yeah." He nodded. "Of course. I guess I'm just stressed from work, that's all."

22. No Fleabag, Please

While I was grateful we were both on the same page again, I wished he'd said something about not being able to live without me.

* * *

A few weeks after we'd settled into our new home, Jack and I invited a small group of friends over to celebrate our new digs. He insisted on taking care of everything and seemed in his element as the party planner. He took care of the music, set the lighting, and bought enough cheese, fruit, and fresh veggies to last for days. Before the first guest arrived, he entered the living room wearing his Thierry Mugler suit. The sight of him sent a flurry of heat down south.

I was excited to see my friends and meet his, but I couldn't wait to show off my new, updated style to Angel. Her fashion sense came naturally. Me? I had to work at looking cool, and even then, some of my fashion choices were questionable.

The moment she arrived with her husband, Angel stood back and took in the new me. "Darling, is that all your own hair?"

"Can you believe it?" I said, turning around so she could see my new style. "Jack took me to his stylist."

"You look completely different." Angel reached out to touch my curls.

"He picked out this dress too." I twirled to show off my new, short, tight little black dress, almost tripping in my black heels. I felt like one of the trendy PIBs I used to want to hang out with at parties.

"I like your new look," Angel said, "but you shouldn't have to change yourself for someone ... outside or in."

I heard what she'd said but chose to ignore it.

Later that night, I caught up with Angel and her husband.

John eyed the food and said, "Your new boyfriend is an excellent host."

We walked over to the buffet and watched as John piled a plate with cheese and crackers.

"He's an excellent boyfriend too," I said.

"I'm a bit worried about that," he added.

"About what?"

"He doesn't like his job very much," John said. "Makes me wonder, would he be a good provider? You've got to stop playing around, Susan, and start thinking about your future."

"I thought I was," I said, looking at Angel for help. I thought she'd given me her blessing when the two of us met Jack at church. "At least he's got a job, and he doesn't drink. Besides, he's crazy for me."

125

I'm Not Single, I Have a Dog

Angel grabbed my hand. "Darling, I encouraged you to get to know him first, be friends, remember?"

"Yes, I remember."

"It's not just the job," John chimed in again. "It's his attitude. He's a fun guy, a party boy. You don't marry the fun guy. You don't start a family with the party boy. You need to ask yourself, is this man capable of providing for a family?"

"But I'm in love." My heart dropped.

"Love is not enough in this world," Angel said. "Sure, he's nice. But after spending time with him, John and I don't believe he'd make a good husband for you. He's just not responsible enough."

My stomach dropped. Deep down inside, I knew they were right. I'd observed Jack's insecurity and fear of commitment for myself. I never understood why he hadn't gone through with marrying his longtime girlfriend. And why had he come up with those stupid reasons not to move in with me? Then, there was his myriad of complaints about his job. The fact that it didn't pay very well made matters worse. Hell, I made more money than Jack did.

At the end of the party, I wondered if I'd made another gigantic relationship mistake.

* * *

I knew living with someone meant compromise. That was why I offered my fashionista beau the large walk-in closet. I placed my wardrobe in the extra room along with my dresser. I also used the bathroom in the hall, leaving the master to my man. Moving in with Jack also meant I became sleep deprived. Jack snored. Loud enough to keep both me and Blondie up all night.

"You slept on the couch again?" Jack asked one morning, wearing his nightly uniform—tighty-whities.

"Yes, Sir Snores-a-Lot," I said. "I've never felt this tired."

By then, we'd been living together for several months. For me, that meant four months without getting any REM sleep.

"I'm thinking about putting another bed in the extra room for me."

"Don't do that," he said, moving in for a morning kiss. "Just wake me, and I'll take the couch next time."

My chance to take him up on his offer came that very night.

"You're snoring," I said, gently nudging him.

Jack rolled over and snored even louder.

"Hey, wake up."

126

22. No Fleabag, Please

This time, I shoved him in the arm, but the racket kept going.

"Snore, snore, snore!" I yelled at him.

He opened his eyes. "What are you doing?" he asked.

Before I could answer, he rolled onto his back, and the noise began again, only louder.

I tried throwing a glass of water on him, but it didn't work. The water ended up running onto my side of the bed. I got no sleep that night.

*   *   *

Before bed the next evening, I asked Jack if we could talk about the issue. "I don't understand. You never snored like this before we moved in together," I said.

"It comes and goes, I guess. Might be sleep apnea."

"You think? Why don't you go to the doctor?"

"I did once. He said I have to have a sleep study and all this stuff. Too much of a hassle for me."

"Well, your snoring is a big hassle for me," I said. "You've kept me up just about every night. Why don't you just take the couch? There's not enough room for me and Blondie anyway."

"I won't snore tonight," Jack said, "and if I do, I promise I'll move."

So much for his promises. Right on cue, the next night, he snored so loudly that I jumped out of bed.

"If you don't stop, I'm going to put your bass in the hallway." I figured he'd never let anything happen to his bass. "If it gets stolen, it's your fault."

His answer? Even louder snoring.

I stomped to the closet, grabbed his guitar, placed his prized possession in the hallway outside of our apartment, and then came back inside and headed to the couch. I lay there, fuming. On top of my lack of sleep, I also felt guilty. *What if someone took his guitar?* I brought it back inside.

The next day, I bought a second bed.

*   *   *

I took over the extra room once the new bed arrived. My stuff was already in that room. I didn't realize our relationship would suffer when I moved into my own room, but it did. In no time, we became more like roommates than lovers. But I finally got some much-needed sleep.

"I'm taking you out to dinner for your birthday," Jack told me one night. A year had already passed.

I'm Not Single, I Have a Dog

I figured we'd go to one of our usual spots and enjoy a meal together. After the move, a low-key celebration seemed like a good idea. I only wished Blondie could join us.

When the big day arrived, I got dressed up in my one of my new wardrobe stables that Jack had encouraged me to buy—my basic black dress. I spent hours getting my hair to look like it had after seeing his stylist. Jack wore black jeans, his Rolling Stones tee, and a leather jacket.

"Where are we going?" I asked.

"You'll know soon enough," he said.

"I love surprises," I said.

When he pulled into the parking lot at the House of Blues, I realized this was going to be anything but low-key.

"You got us passes to the Foundation Room?"

It was a private VIP area. I'd only been in there once before with Angel. She knew everyone.

"Sure did," he said. "And The Cars are playing."

"I've always loved The Cars," I said. "Part of the backdrop soundtrack to my college days."

We walked into the crowded lounge, holding hands. Jack led me to a secret room reserved only for the biggest VIPs.

I squeezed his hand. I couldn't wait to see what celebs might be hanging out there.

"Surprise!" my friends shouted.

Everyone I loved was there—except Angel, who I knew was out of town. Jack had managed to even get my brother, Will, to come.

A waiter placed a glass of champagne in my hand.

"It's your favorite—Cristal," Jack said, puffing up his chest.

I had to ask him, "How'd you get us in here?"

"I called Angel," he said. "She's a member and called the club, I told your friends, and here we are."

"I can't believe you did this for me," I said.

"Of course." He looked me in the eyes. "I'd do anything for you. I love you."

Jack planted a big kiss on me right there in front of everyone. I'd finally found my man.

When the band started to play their hit "Just What I Needed," I realized Jack was just what I needed. The evening was magical.

At the end of the night, the waiter gave Jack the bill.

"Here's some money," my brother, Will, pulled out a hundred-dollar bill.

22. No Fleabag, Please

Other guests handed Jack cash but not nearly enough to pay for the pricy night.

When Jack went to pull out his wallet, he came up empty-handed.

"No, no, no, no. Fuck no," he said.

"What's wrong?" I asked.

Jack grabbed me. "I can't find my wallet." His eyes were wide.

"Let's retrace your steps," I suggested, but he became frantic.

"Everything's in there—my money, my credit cards."

"Don't worry; we'll take care of this." I pulled out my credit card and gave it to the waiter. "You can use this card for whatever the cash doesn't cover," I told him.

Everyone left, but Jack and I spent the next hour searching the Foundation Room for his damn wallet. But it was nowhere to be found.

23

You Had Me at Woof

"The world looks different to me," I told Jack one cloudy Saturday morning while he was washing his car in the driveway. "Colors are brighter; everything looks fresh, new, and exciting. Even going to the DMV with you yesterday was an adventure. I've never felt like this before."

"Glad to hear it. That's what you're supposed to feel when you're in love." Jack threw his sponge in a bucket and stood to give me a kiss. "We do make a good team. Thanks for canceling all my credit cards ... again."

Jack was always losing something. This was the second time in six months for his wallet to end up missing. Luckily, I'd kept his information from the last time.

"Why are you washing your car today?" I looked up at the big, dark clouds floating above us. "It's about to rain."

"Yeah," he muttered, "just my luck."

"Are you okay, sweetie?"

He loved that old car of his and spent hours cleaning it by hand every weekend, polishing the deep blue finish so it reflected like a mirror.

"I always do such stupid things." He rubbed a soapy sponge over the hood.

"What do you mean?"

"Losing my wallet, misplacing my keys. Seems something is always missing."

"Don't be so hard on yourself. You're doing the best you can, right?"

"It's my stupid job," he said. "My boss is driving me crazy."

"That's what bosses do. Just let it go."

"I can't." He hosed off the soap. "He's an ass."

"Well, it's the weekend, and you don't have to think about it today."

"You're right," he sighed. "But I do have to drop off my dry cleaning."

"Great. I've got some errands to run too. I'll run upstairs and get your dry cleaning and my purse."

23. You Had Me at Woof

Blondie hated to get wet, so I decided to leave her where she was, sleeping on the bathroom floor.

* * *

Jack parked the car outside our local dry cleaner, got out of the car, and opened the back door to get his clothes. I waited in the car, listening to a new R.E.M. CD. I closed my eyes, and a sudden jolt rocked the car. I turned off the stereo. Someone had hit the car. My first thought was how upset Jack would be.

I got out and looked around but didn't see Jack. Cars had stopped in every direction. The driver of the one facing me looked shocked, his mouth wide open, eyes wide, cell phone to his ear. The world became silent and went into slow motion. I walked around the car. Jack lay motionless, facedown, arms stretched on the asphalt above his head.

"Jack!" I sat on the street next to him. "Don't you leave me."

Blood formed a pool beside his head. I took off my coat and held it over his body. The dark clouds that had threatened earlier opened up. Rain pelted onto the street, and Jack's blood washed away like a memory.

I heard sirens. Help was on the way. But Jack hadn't moved. I couldn't tell if he was breathing or not. I held my breath.

As soon as the paramedics arrived, Jack jumped to his feet like a jack-in-the-box.

"My head, my shoulder, my knee," he said, pacing and moaning in pain.

The owner of the dry cleaner brought out a chair and set it next to Jack on the pavement.

"Sir, we need you to sit down," a paramedic said.

Jack paced. "My head, my shoulder, my knee," he repeated.

The paramedics placed him onto a gurney and loaded him into the ambulance.

"We're taking him to Cedars-Sinai Medical Center," the paramedic said.

I brushed the tears and rain from my face. "Can I ride with him?"

"No, just meet us at the emergency room."

Jack's car seemed fine, so I got behind the wheel to follow the ambulance. Turned out, the only damage on the car was to the driver's side mirror. *Would Jack be okay?*

At Cedars, I parked the car and ran into the emergency room. It was packed. So crowded that no one stopped me when I ran past the check-in counter to find the love of my life.

I found Jack lying on a gurney in the hallway. He was a bloody mess. Blood dripped from his forehead, and his right eye was swollen shut.

I stood there in the chaos and prayed as Jack went in and out of consciousness.

He woke up and said, "An angel with red hair asked me if I was ready to go to the light."

I kissed his forehead. "Tell that angel to go away."

"Did I do something wrong?" he asked.

"No, honey. When you grabbed your clothes from the backseat, a car hit you," I said.

His doctor arrived and examined him right there in the hall.

"Did you witness the accident?" he asked, shining a light into Jack's eye—the one that wasn't swollen shut.

"I didn't see it, but I heard it."

"How long has he been unconscious?"

"He's been going in and out since he got hit," I said. "I'd say he was completely out for a good five minutes before the paramedics got there. Seemed like hours to me."

"We need to run some tests," the doctor said.

An orderly appeared to wheel Jack away from me. I watched them disappear down the hall.

"You're lucky he came here," the doctor said. "We've got an entire ward dedicated to brain injury."

"Brain injury?"

"I'll make sure you get updates," the doctor said and then ran off to catch up with the gurney carrying my boyfriend.

I headed for the waiting room, but a nurse stopped before I got there.

"Are you his wife?" she asked.

"No, but I'm his live-in girlfriend."

"Good. I need to ask you some questions." She grabbed her clipboard.

"Is he allergic to any medication?"

"I don't think so," I said. "The doctor said something about his brain?" I caught my breath. *What if Jack had brain damage?*

"We don't know the extent of his injuries yet. Does he have any immediate family?"

"Yes, he has a brother he's close to, but I don't have my phone book with me."

"We'll need that number as soon as possible."

"We live close by," I said. "I'll run over and get it."

23. You Had Me at Woof

On the way out, two policemen stopped me.

"Miss, can we get a statement from you?" one of them asked.

My head was spinning. "I didn't see anything, just heard a loud bump and then saw my boyfriend lying in the street. There were lots of witnesses, though."

"Yeah," said the other officer. "Two private citizens followed the driver that hit Jack, stopped him, and placed him under citizen's arrest. The guy has no insurance."

My stomach churned.

"Take this card," the officer said. "Call us if you think of anything."

I turned to leave but was stopped again by the doctor.

"He's going to need knee surgery. Looks like he also has a shoulder fracture. We're checking on possible swelling in his skull. We're admitting him to the brain injury ward."

I suddenly felt very small. "Sounds serious."

"If the swelling gets much worse, we're going to have to drill holes in his skull to alleviate it," he said.

Once I got back in Jack's car, I couldn't hold back my tears. I hugged the steering wheel and sat there for a long time.

At home, I went on autopilot. First, I found my phone book. Next, I walked Blondie. Before I headed back to the hospital, I fed her. And since I didn't know how long I would be at the hospital, I brought Blondie along for the ride. The back of my car was like a kennel with a dog bed and plenty of water. Blondie comforted me and gave me strength, and the last thing I wanted was to be on my own.

*   *   *

I stayed at the hospital until the wee hours of the morning, checking on Blondie every hour. A nurse finally reported that besides his knee and shoulder injuries, Jack had also suffered a basilar skull fracture, had a serious concussion, and a hematoma that had caused the swelling in his skull.

"There's nothing more you can do here," the nurse said. "Why don't you head home and get some sleep?"

I followed her suggestion and managed to get a few hours of sleep.

Although I woke up dog-tired, I still managed to make it to work the next morning on time. I acted as if nothing had happened, afraid that if I didn't, I might lose my job if I shared my personal drama. I'd seen others be forced out that way. The company didn't like its employees to bring their issues to the workplace. The office was similar to the home I grew up in—only share the happy, bury the sad.

I couldn't let that happen. I even drove to a meeting in the City of Industry that day, about an hour away. The client? A sardine company. Try doing public relations for sardines after your boyfriend got run over by a car.

I pretended to be fine. Visiting Jack every night after work was the highlight of my day.

Two weeks into his hospital stay, Jack asked, "When am I getting out of here?"

"Soon," I answered.

It didn't take a brain surgeon to tell Jack was in a lot of pain. But thank God the swelling on his brain had started to dissipate.

"You don't need brain surgery," I told him. "That's a good thing, right?"

"Yeah," he said, "At least I've got that going for me."

The day Jack was discharged, I heard his neurologist tell Jack, "You're lucky you don't have permanent brain damage." Jack could have easily become a vegetable or worse.

The thought of losing him forever made me want to hold on tight. I craved romance and commitment, but in reality, Jack became more of a companion, someone to care for in addition to my dog.

24

Dog-Tired

Over the next year, Jack recovered in a rented hospital bed set up in the middle of our living room. Due to his injuries, Jack was unable to work, which meant I paid for everything. His knee injury didn't allow him to stand for long periods of time, so as well as working harder, I prepared all meals, did our grocery shopping and laundry, and became his official chauffeur, taking him to his many appointments. Basically, I became Jack's caretaker.

Luckily, his doctors and physical therapists were all located in the same high-rise building not far from my office, which made life a bit easier. The most difficult issue for me was keeping my patience. It took Jack forever to get out of the house. Besides having to hobble on crutches, he always forgot something, and I had to go back upstairs and get whatever he'd left behind. I spent a lot of time waiting and backtracking.

One morning, I pulled up to the curb to drop him off for his physical therapy appointment. From there, he was scheduled to check in with his doctor, followed by a massage. Oh, how I needed a massage!

"Can you call someone else for a ride home?" I asked. "I'm slammed at work right now."

My client list had grown to include three luxury resorts outside Palm Springs, and I was leaving the next morning for my first media familiarization trip—or, as it was referred to in the industry, a media FAM.

"Like who?" Jack said. "I don't see people knocking down the door to help us out."

I knew Jack was estranged from his sisters and mother, but he did have a relationship with his younger brother, another gifted musician, although he couldn't always be counted on. He had a list of issues too long to count.

"Come on, Jack," I sighed. "I've got twenty journalists flying in from all over the country tomorrow for that media FAM. They're all high-maintenance."

"Okay." He sulked. "Guess I can walk home."

Considering his doctor's office was several miles from our home, walking was not an option.

"Don't be ridiculous. I'll give you some money for a cab." I reached into my wallet, but it was empty. "I don't have any cash on me. Do you?"

"What do you think? I'm not working right now," he said. "I can't afford to take cabs."

"Oh, fuck it. Call me when you're ready. I'll pick you up, but remember, you're on your own as of tomorrow. I'll be gone on that press trip."

"Which is why I didn't schedule any appointments while you're away."

He slammed the car door, and I rolled down the window.

"We need to figure out another way to get you to and from your appointments."

"I know," Jack said. "I'll come up with a solution."

* * *

The phone on my desk was ringing when I got to the office. I answered it before I sat down.

"You'd like an additional scalp massage?" I asked a reporter from a leading spa magazine, searching for a pen to add the request to my growing list of things to do. "I'm sure we can fit that in."

I scribbled a note and sat down in time to pick up the next call.

"Sure, we can change your flight," I said to the writer from *USA Today*, her third request for a change in her itinerary. "Not a problem." I made a note in my trusty notebook.

The moment I hung up, the phone rang again.

I listened while another reporter shared a concern.

"Yes, we have you down as a vegetarian," I told him. "Oh, you're eating meat now?"

Every detail of the trip had to be seamless. And they were all left up to me, no one else.

I answered another call.

"Hi, Susan," another journalist sweetly spoke into the phone. "Do I need to bring a sweater?"

I rolled my eyes and listened to more ridiculous questions. "Well, it can get chilly at night, so I'd say yes, bring a sweater."

I hung up and said under my breath, "Should I come over and pack for you too?"

The calls kept coming—and not only regarding the media FAM. I also had to take care of my other clients. I usually liked being busy but maybe not this busy. Still, time flew by. I couldn't leave my desk, afraid I'd miss an important call.

"This is Susan. Can you hold, please?" I put a call on hold to pick up another.

Before I could say anything, Mom said, "This is your mother, who loves you." She had a habit of calling at the worst possible moment. "I need you to come over after work and change a lightbulb."

"Mom, this is not the best time...."

My parents were aging. Dad suffered from the early stages of Parkinson's disease, and he and Mom seemed to constantly be in need of my help.

"And listen," Mom continued, "I got rid of that Meals on Wheels thingy, so don't pay for it anymore. The food was awful."

"What?" I asked, forgetting I'd put someone on hold. "First, you fire the caretaker Will and I hired to help you with Dad, and now, this. I can't run out there all the time. It takes forever to get over the hill in traffic."

Mom never called my brother, Will, for help even though he lived a lot closer than me. He'd just tied the knot, and because he was a newly-wed, Mom didn't want to bother him. My married sister, Erin, lived in Northern California and was busy with her own career and raising two girls. But I, the youngest, the unwed daughter, was fair game.

"I've got to take this other call. I'll see you around six."

I hung up with Mom to pick up the other line.

"Where are you?" Jack said, frantic. "I've been calling you for the last half hour. I need a ride home."

"Oh my God! I'm sorry. It's been one of those days. I haven't had time to pee. I'll be right there."

* * *

After working overtime, chauffeuring Jack around, and traveling over the hill to change a lightbulb for Mom, I came home to pack for my first ever media FAM. I planned to leave at five the next morning, miss rush hour, and make it to Palm Springs in two hours.

Jack lay in his hospital bed, the television blaring.

"I left you some frozen dinners," I said, "and lots of healthy snacks."

"Frozen dinners?"

"Yep. I figured they would be the easiest for you while I'm away. And don't forget that I hired our neighbor to walk Blondie. But you'll have to feed her while I'm gone. And make sure she has water."

"Yes, ma'am," he said.

He knew I hated to be called ma'am, but I ignored his jab.

* * *

At five a.m., I turned onto the 405, turned up the radio, and headed east to the 101 to catch the 110. With no traffic, I made good time. Some of the journalists were waiting in the lobby at the Marriott Rancho Las Palmas, my client for this press trip.

"You're here already?" I really wanted to take a few moments to gather my thoughts before embarking on our grueling three-day schedule. Anything could happen. Being in charge of a group of journalists, all with their own agendas, was not an easy task.

"They're saying we can't check in yet," the reporter from *USA Today* said.

"Let me get that fixed," I said, staying positive. "Meantime, why don't you all meet me in the main restaurant for breakfast?"

I wasn't planning on having my client host breakfast on the first day but hey, they screwed up the reservations.

I ran ahead of the travel and spa journalists to let the restaurant know the new plan. After introducing myself, I asked the hostess to seat the group of VIPs right away. They were perusing the menus while I ran to the front desk to take care of their early check-in.

After breakfast, I took them on a Jeep ride in the desert. We stopped at a new restaurant in town for lunch and ended the day with a gourmet meal.

On day two, I had a little break. We met for breakfast, and then I sent all the journalists to the new resort spa for massages. I didn't have another group activity planned until that night when we were meeting with the resort chef for another gourmet meal. That meant I got to enjoy a little much-needed me time. I decided to start with a power nap.

I had just drifted off to sleep when the phone rang.

"We don't know what to do," the spa director told me. "The editor of *Spa Magazine* is ... well ... how do I put this? He smells."

"Smells? What do you mean?"

"The masseuse said she can't even enter the room," she said. "He smells of stale cigarettes, sweat, and wine. I guess all that wine he drank last night is seeping through his pores."

"I guess so. But what can I do about it?"

"Do you have any suggestions about how to handle this?"

"Sounds like he needs to bathe." I remembered touring the facility, and some of the treatment rooms included showers. "How about telling him the treatment starts with a shower?"

"That's an excellent idea," she said. "I'll tell her now."

I couldn't get back to sleep after we hung up, so I headed to the spa to make sure everything was fine. My idea worked, and the journalist remained clueless. Crisis resolved.

The rest of the trip went smoothly, except for one small hiccup at dinner the last night when we were short one table setting.

I asked one of the writers who was seated at the end of the long table, "Do you mind moving over?"

She slid her chair only an inch and then said, "I'm left-handed."

I didn't know why that mattered, but I let it go. I turned to the journalist seated on the other side of the table and asked her for help.

"No problem," she said.

Once we were all seated, the five-course food show began. The trip ended that night with full tummies and lots to write about. I would have to follow up with everyone back at the office, but I felt confident the trip would result in positive stories about the resort and spa.

The freeway on the way home was bumper-to-bumper traffic, which gave me a little time to contemplate the trip. I thought being in charge of a media FAM would be fun, but in reality, I'd had to babysit a group of self-absorbed travel writers who expected the moon and more. I couldn't wait to put my feet up and kiss my dog.

"Welcome back," Jack said.

Blondie greeted me with her signature wiggle. Her paws were filthy, and black prints were smeared all over the carpet.

"What happened to Blondie?"

"I took her on a walk," Jack said. "She got in some mud."

"Thanks for taking care of her for me."

I took a peek into the kitchen. Rice was all over the floor, dirty dishes were stacked in the sink, and trash was on the counter.

I sat down and put my head in my hands. It wasn't his fault, but still. After caring for a bunch of entitled strangers, I felt depleted.

Out of the corner of my eye, I saw Blondie walking toward me. She always comforted me. But this time was different. She was walking funny, sort of sideways. Before she got to me, she leaned over and fell to the ground.

"Blondie, what's wrong?" I tried not to freak out.

She got up and wobbled, only to fall again.

"Jack, we've got to get her to the vet now."

Jack held Blondie in his lap on the way to the vet. He petted her, kissed her on the top of the head, and let her stick her head out the window.

"You're gonna be all right, girl," he said.

That's the man I fell in love with.

When we reached the parking lot, I told Jack, "You stay here."

I carefully took Blondie in my arms to carry her inside.

We were rushed into a room, ahead of the other patients in the waiting room.

"I don't know what happened," I told Dr. Winters. "Out of nowhere, she started to wobble, her head tilted, and she fell over."

He sat on the tile floor next to her. "Looks like she had a doggie stroke."

"I didn't know dogs could have strokes," I said. "Will she be okay?"

"The neurologic signs associated with a stroke usually resolve on their own," he said, his voice comforting. "We'll give her some steroids to help her body reestablish blood flow and reduce swelling." He turned to prepare the shot.

I kissed Blondie on the forehead. "You're going to be okay, girlie girl."

When we returned to the car, Jack asked, "She okay?"

I gently placed her in his arms. "She had a doggie stroke."

"I didn't know that could happen to dogs," he said.

"Me either. Turns out, they're not very common in dogs. He gave her a shot."

"Poor little Blondie." He hugged her.

"He told me she'd rally. Do you think she'll rally?"

"I hope so," Jack said. "You'll rally, right, Blondie?"

*   *   *

Blondie snuggled close to me all night. I got the feeling she was scared. By the morning, my baby girl still had trouble walking, but she was no longer falling over. Still, I couldn't stand to see my baby so weak.

"Come here, girlie. Let's talk." I sat on the floor beside her.

"I'm not ready for you to die." I placed her head in my lap and stroked her back. "If you have to, I understand. I'm sure there is lots of turkey in heaven. But if you stay here with me, I promise to give you turkey every day."

24. Dog-Tired

Blondie must have understood me because she did rally later that day, just like the vet had said she would. And I kept my promise to her, giving her turkey every single day.

With Blondie out of the woods, I vowed to put Susan at the top of my list. I was determined to love myself as much as my dog loved me.

25

Bark! The Herald Angels Sing

The Christmas of '98 was quiet. No celebrations, no parties. With Jack still recovering from the accident, I tried my best to get him into the holiday spirit. I hung Christmas ornaments from the ceiling in the living room and set up a small living tree on the fireplace mantel. The plant's plastic container was covered with colorful wrapping paper. I could replant it in a big pot later to grow on our balcony until next year.

Underneath, I placed the presents. On Christmas Eve, I lit the gas fireplace, turned out all the lights, and strategically placed candles around the living room to set the mood.

We were both exhausted from everything—Jack recovering from major head trauma, a shoulder fracture, the pending knee surgery, and me recovering from life. That evening, we fell asleep—Jack in his hospital bed, me on the couch.

"Susan! Wake up! Fire!" Jack yelled.

I woke out of a deep sleep.

Through my sleepy haze, I saw the flames. The candles I'd lit earlier had set the little Christmas tree's plastic container on fire. Molten plastic dripped all over the packages below, which were now in flames.

I jumped to my feet and grabbed the Christmas tree.

"Shit!"

The plastic singed my fingers and caused me to drop the burning mess on top of the presents.

Jack yelled, "Throw it in the kitchen sink, not there."

"I'm trying."

I tried to grab the tree again, but Jack jumped to his feet and grabbed it. He ran as best as he could into the kitchen. I followed him and watched as he sprang into action, propping himself up against the sink, dousing the tree and handing me a pan filled with water.

"Here," he said. "Take this and throw water on the flames. Quick!"

I did as he said. The water helped douse the flames, but one pan wasn't going to do the trick.

"More!" I yelled, running back to the kitchen.

I ran my burned fingers under cold water and noticed my new holiday velvet blouse was covered in tiny burn holes. Jack came out unscathed.

Once we heard the sizzle and saw the smoke that meant the fire was out, we sat down next to each other in total shock.

"Why didn't the fire alarms go off?" Jack asked.

"I have no idea, but if you hadn't woken up, the entire building could have been destroyed and us with it, Blondie too."

The phone rang, startling both of us back to reality.

Did this really just happen?

"Hello?" I said.

Once again, Mom had called at the worst possible moment.

"Listen, your father had a fall and hurt his hip. I took him to the doctor. After an X-ray, they admitted him. We're at Northridge Hospital."

"I'll be right there."

"My dad's in the hospital," I told Jack. "He fell again. I've got to get over there right away."

"Oh no," Jack said. "I hope he's okay. I'd go with you, but I have band practice."

"I know. I'll see you later."

* * *

I grabbed Blondie and my purse and raced downstairs to my car. The freeway was jammed, and it took me an hour and a half to get to the hospital.

I parked in the hospital's parking structure and left Blondie in the car while I headed inside. I found Mom sitting with Dad in his hospital room.

Mom looked up when I entered. "The doctors found an aortic aneurysm."

"I have to have it fixed," Dad said. "I've got a lot more life to live."

I leaned over and kissed his forehead. "Of course you do. You're a fighter."

"It'll mean a long recovery, if I even make it through the surgery."

Mom stood stoic, her hardened exterior exposed.

I looked at Dad; he seemed frail. "You'll survive; you're a strong man."

In truth, Dad wasn't the man he used to be, and I had concerns about him getting through the surgery, but I did my best to stay positive for his sake. He'd already gone through two open heart surgeries … and now this.

"Your dad filled out an advance directive, just in case," Mom said. "We want you to know we're leaving the house to you."

"Mom, quit being so dramatic. Dad'll be fine, and you're not goin' anywhere."

She went on, "Will has a house, Erin has a house, and we want to make sure you have one too."

"Stop talking like that," I said.

"Will and Erin will split our savings and stocks," Dad added.

"Both of you, stop. Do Will and Erin even know you're in the hospital?"

"I called them," Mom answered. "Your brother said he'd try to get here later."

Will showed up the next day. Erin was a no-show. As always, I jumped to the rescue.

We scheduled the surgery.

* * *

I stopped for fast food on the way home, and Blondie was thrilled to get a hamburger.

"Here you go." I blew on it to make sure she wouldn't burn her pink doggie tongue. "Life's got to get better than this."

I got home quickly, around ten p.m. There was no traffic at that hour. Jack stood outside, waiting for us, so I parked in front of my building to talk to him, forgoing my usual parking space in the security garage. I had to let Blondie go potty anyway.

She got busy and sniffed the bushes. She didn't even notice Jack.

"How is he?" Jack asked, limping toward me.

"Not good." I sniffed. "He has to have major surgery."

Jack embraced me.

We stood on the sidewalk, waiting for Blondie to finish her business when an old beat-up jalopy screeched around the corner and stopped directly in front of us. The passenger door flew open; a tall man stepped out, holding a gun pointed at me.

"Ohhh nooo." I heard a strange gasp come out of me but couldn't take in the gravity of the situation. Jack stood stiff.

The man with the gun walked toward me. His eyes bulged. I smelled the acrid, sweaty, sharp scent of fear, not clear if it was coming from me or from the gunman. His pupils were dilated. His body twitched. I froze.

He got close to us and cracked his neck. "Gimme that purse." He pointed the gun straight at my forehead.

I couldn't move, thinking about my new Coach bag with my new lipstick. *What was the name of that shade? And what about my favorite pen? I loved that Tiffany pen; it was a present from a client.*

"Give it to him," Jack said. The gun touched my forehead. "Susan, give him your damn purse."

In slow motion, I handed my purse to the wild-eyed man. He grabbed it and then turned the gun to Jack.

"Now, both of you, turn around slow-like and walk inside."

I heard his words but didn't follow his instructions. Instead, I moved forward. I had to rescue Blondie.

"I said, turn around!"

Jack grabbed my hand, "Where are you going?"

"I need to get Blondie," I said.

Jack spun me around toward the entrance. "She'll be okay, but we could get shot."

Once we were safely behind the gate, we heard a car screech off into the night.

My mouth dried, my breathing was shallow, and my teeth chattered like crazy. I broke down, shaking out of control, and fell to my knees.

"Hey, what are you doing now?" Jack said. He helped me up and sat me on a patio chair. "Stay here."

Jack headed to the front of the building. Seconds later, he walked back inside, carrying Blondie.

"She didn't notice a thing," he said and placed her in my arms. "She was still sniffing that same bush."

Blondie looked up at me as if to say, *What's wrong?*

I held her close until my breathing slowed, and the shaking stopped. Jack took my hand in his, and the three of us headed back inside to call the police.

26

Lucky Dogs?

When Jack became strong enough, we took our first vacation together since his accident. We planned to take the long, scenic route to San Francisco. I wanted to bring Blondie along, but he didn't.

"I don't want to travel with a dog," Jack said, "just us."

"She has a name. Blondie won't be any trouble. Besides, I don't know anyone who I could leave her with."

"What about Angel?" Jack asked.

"She's got four dogs of her own," I answered, "and two kids and a husband. I can't ask her to do that."

Truth? I didn't want to leave Blondie behind. By that time, my sweet dog's old age meant bathroom accidents in the house were an everyday occurrence. I'd never boarded her before, and the thought of leaving her in a crate or kennel for a week at age eighteen seemed cruel. But in the end, I compromised my needs for Jack and talked Mom and Dad into looking after Blondie. My parents wouldn't crate her, and she'd have the run of the house and the huge backyard.

Jack was eager to check out the music scene in San Francisco and wanted to hit all the bars and clubs he could during our time in the city. I enjoyed music, but the thought of clubbing every night didn't sound relaxing. I imagined us picnicking at Golden Gate Park, exploring Chinatown, walking around Fisherman's Wharf. I looked forward to the Amish quilt exhibit at the de Young Museum in Golden Gate Park.

"We have to check out the big hair and blue Mohawks at Club DV8," he said. "Not a live music place, but I hear they play lots of techno, new wave, alternative. You're going to love it."

"If I go with you to that club, will you check out the Amish exhibit with me tomorrow?"

"Of course."

He never made it to the quilts, but I went one morning while Jack slept in. When I returned, he was still in bed.

26. Lucky Dogs?

"Wake up, sleepyhead," I said.

"Leave me alone," Jack said. "I'm on vacation."

"Yeah, you're at club bed. Come on. It's so beautiful outside. Let's go explore."

I tried to keep from nagging him, especially since Jack had told me that was what had ruined his long-term relationship. I rationalized that his former girlfriend hadn't nurtured him the way I could.

I opened the curtains.

"Don't...." he growled and then rolled over. "I'm resting for tonight."

"Well, you rest up," I said. "I'll see you later."

I grabbed my bag, put on my sunglasses, and headed outside for fun. My destination? Golden Gate Park. I had my taxi driver drop me off at the park entrance and walked toward the de Young Museum. I saw the museum's twisting tower rising above the canopy of trees surrounding it. With the blue sky above sprinkled with fluffy white clouds, the scene looked like a Maxfield Parrish painting.

"Breathtaking," I said to myself. "Wish I'd brought Blondie. She would've loved this place."

The Amish quilt exhibit was every bit as interesting as I'd hoped. Not long before the trip, I had done a little geological research and learned that my ancestor Jacob Hartzler was the first Amish bishop to colonize the United States in 1749.

Quilts hung on the museum walls like paintings by modern artists. Most of the collection featured traditional quilt designs, some dating back to the middle of the eighteenth century.

The exhibit did not only offer a feast for the eyes, but it also included historic details about the Amish. I was surprised to learn that the Amish had come to the United States to escape religious oppression in Europe.

Then I read that the women who had created these works of art purposely planned a mistake into each of their projects because they believed attempts at human perfection mocked God.

That got me thinking about my relationship with Jack. I had defiantly made my share of mistakes with him, but it seemed like being with him meant forgetting about myself. I finally realized Jack was never going to change, and it wasn't up to me to change him. I realized at that moment that somewhere over the past few years, I'd stopped doing what made me happy in order to do what made Jack happy. And maybe that was why I preferred my dog to my man. Anything I did with her made me happy.

I'm Not Single, I Have a Dog

* * *

During the drive back to LA, Jack and I argued—a lot. In the middle of yelling about God knew what, I heard on the radio that John Pratt had died from AIDS.

"What? How could that be? I just saw them last week." My entire body was taken over by gut-wrenching pain. "Nooo!" I screamed.

"I'm sorry, Susan." Jack put his right hand on my knee.

"I've got to get to Angel's right away," I said, shaking. "She must be devastated."

"But you said you'd go to my friend's party," Jack reminded me.

"I can't go to a party. My friend's husband just died."

"Come on, just for an hour," he pleaded. "It'll be fun."

"I don't think I can be in a room of strangers right now," I said. "I need to see my friend."

"I know, but can't you just take a moment to meet my friends first?"

Before Jack could introduce me to his friend, the hostess, I asked if I could use her phone. Jack headed out back to join the fun while I disappeared into the bedroom to call Angel.

"Angel, I'm so sorry. What happened?"

To my surprise, Angel sounded calm. "Darling, I'll tell you everything when I see you. Don't rush. Everyone's here. I'm fine."

Jack knew I loved John and Angel and that I'd want to comfort my dear friend as soon as possible. *How could he be so insensitive and inconsiderate?* I sank into a pit of sadness and waited in the car.

* * *

The moment we got home, I rushed to see Angel. She sat in her living room, surrounded by friends. I knew them all, had attended many parties and dinners with them, but for some reason, my friendship with Angel remained separate.

"I'm shocked," I said.

"I know, darling. John wanted to keep it secret."

"I understand. I'm a publicist, after all."

I remembered receiving a phone call a few months prior from a friend who worked at *Entertainment Tonight*. I'd thought it was strange when she asked, "Is John Pratt dying?"

John had exercised every day, he had eaten well, and he had looked healthy to the end. Later, I read that Angel wore disguises when she visited her husband at Cedars-Sinai Medical Center. They'd kept the entire ordeal secret, out of the news.

26. Lucky Dogs?

"I don't know what to say," I said, hugging Angel.

"Come with me." She took me by the hand and headed to her bedroom, leaving her other friends in the living room. "Please, tell me about you. How'd the vacation go?"

I shook my head and held back tears. "Angel, I don't want to talk about myself. Seems silly next to what you're going through."

"That's the point. I need to hear about something positive."

"I don't know how positive I can be." I managed a smile. "Jack and I argued the entire time. We were like an old couple who'd been together for years, constantly bickering at each other."

"Arguing is normal, darling." She picked up a framed photo of John from her nightstand. "What's important is the way you both handle those spats. You have to be honest and open with each other. If something's bothering you, you have to let the other person know. That's how John and I made it through all these years."

"How do I let him know he's acting so ... selfish?"

"Difficult conversations aren't easy. But you have to let Jack know how you feel. Even if you don't get to an immediate solution, the fact that you're both willing to listen to each other is what keeps a relationship strong."

"You're so wise," I said. "I'm lucky to have you as my friend."

She placed the frame back on the nightstand. "Treat Jack the same way you treat me, like your friend." Angel's beautiful sky-blue eyes brimmed with tears. "Think about it; best friends are honest and kind. They accept each other the way they are and love each other unconditionally. John was my best friend."

Her tears flowed, and I hugged her.

"From one minute to the next," she said through sobs, "such a whirlwind of emotions."

"I can't even imagine. And I know you so well. I'm sure you're acting strong for your kids, hiding a lot of your hurt inside because you probably think that's what people expect. Just know I don't expect anything. You can call me anytime, day or night. I'll listen."

"I know, darling. You've always been there for me."

That was when I realized that I might not be good at picking the right man, but I sure got blessed in the friend department. And the dog department too.

27

My Pack

Back at my therapist's office I said: "Jack walks around like Pig-Pen in *Peanuts*. You know, the character with a cloud of dirt that surrounds his body and encircles him everywhere he goes. Now that same cloud's hanging over my head."

"You have the power to step away from his black cloud," Beverly said.

"I swear, I've never met anyone with such bad luck."

Beverly raised an eyebrow. "I don't believe in luck. I believe in choices."

"I didn't choose to be robbed at gunpoint," I said. "Wouldn't you know, the one time I had cash on me? I never keep cash."

I sat in the chair across from Beverly—my safe place—so comfortable after seeing her for so many years. She'd become like a mother to me. She knew me intimately, loved me unconditionally. I craved that kind of love in a partner.

"When someone puts a loaded handgun to your forehead, it's profound. You've looked death in the face," she said. "Tell me, how are you feeling?"

"I'd rather forget."

"Don't go there, Susan," she said. "You know the only way out of the darkness is through it."

I grabbed a Kleenex. "It's hard to wrap my mind around what happened. I feel disconnected from my feelings."

"Immediately after a traumatic event, like a robbery, it's common to experience feelings of shock and disbelief," Beverly explained.

My shock seemed to last a long time. I found it hard to let my feelings out when friends encouraged my denial, saying they were impressed by my strength. In truth, strength had nothing to do it. I had become an expert at stuffing my emotions down deep.

Beverly added, "Carl Jung said, 'I am not what happened to me. I am what I choose to become.' You can choose to express your feelings now, or they'll be waiting for you later."

150

"I feel frozen."

"You've been victimized. It's okay to be upset about it."

"I wanna fire a gun, feel the power of a weapon in my hands."

"That's good." Beverly nodded. "That's empowering."

"Jack's been there for me. He took charge, held me all night."

"He's giving you the emotional support and comfort you need."

"He's good in a crisis. Earlier that day, I wanted to break up. Seems like the universe is conspiring to keep us together."

"The universe doesn't dictate who you should be with; don't give your power away. *You* can choose to stay with Jack, but that'll mean lots of compromises."

"I can't imagine compromising more than I already am."

"If you have children with him, you'll still have to work full-time. You can't depend on him to pay the bills."

"That's true."

"I divorced when my kids were young and had to work to support us. It was tough, but we made it through."

"I don't know if I can do that," I said. "I hate to leave my dog when I go to work. I can't imagine leaving my children behind while I head to the office."

"It's all up to you; it's your decision to make. You're young, and you've learned a lot about yourself. Take time to regroup."

"But my biological clock is ticking. Loud!" I said. "Last Sunday, when I received communion at church, I looked back from the altar and saw the kids with their parents and cried."

"Susan, you've got to confront the issue of how you do everything for Jack. He held you that one night, but what about the other times when he's done what he wanted to do? Plus, you told me that you're still paying for everything. All that adds up to a life filled with grief and black clouds."

* * *

I considered my options, as Beverly had recommended, and realized there were many ways to create a family. I didn't have to wait for a man. I could move forward and have a baby on my own. All I needed was sperm.

Jack and I were getting ready to go out to dinner with some friends, bumping into each other in his master bathroom. I turned off my blow dryer and looked him in the eye. I had an important issue to discuss.

"I want to have a baby, Jack."

"I know; you've told me."

"I'm serious," I said.

He shrugged. "Don't look at me. Not interested."

"I can't do it by myself."

"I don't want to be a dad."

"You don't have to. All I need is your sperm. Please say yes."

"I don't know about that." He laughed.

"I'll have documents drawn up, and we'll make it all legal. You've got nothing to lose, except some sperm. I'll take all the responsibility for the child."

"I don't know about jacking off in a cup."

"What are you talking about? Artificial insemination costs thousands of dollars, way too expensive. We'd make a baby the old-fashioned way."

"I can't do that," he said, putting his hands on his hips.

"Why not?" I put down my hairbrush and faced him. "We had sex the other day."

He turned away and said, "Because if you got pregnant after we made love, I'd feel like a dad, legal document or not."

"We could work that out," I said, leaning closer to him. "Anything's possible."

"I'm not ready for a child," he said, turning away from me.

"You're ten years older than me. If not now, when?"

At thirty-nine, I didn't know if I could get pregnant or carry a baby to term. I feared I'd waited too long, wasted my youth.

"You know how much I love kids," Jack said. "But I can't make a baby with you and disappear. Doesn't seem right." He walked out of the bathroom.

"I said we'd work it out; you could be his or her favorite uncle Jack." I followed him.

"You picked the wrong time to have this conversation," Jack said. He grabbed his car keys. "I said, I'll think about being your sperm donor. Now, hurry up, or we'll be late."

Deep down, I knew where my latest request would go with Jack. Nowhere.

* * *

I joined Angel the following week along with a handful of her other friends to help prepare for John's funeral later that day. A genuine sadness lingered around us while we worked, like a palpable cloud of depression.

I'd expected Angel to be all puffy-eyed, carrying around boxes of Kleenex, but my friend looked like a woman getting down to business, not a grieving widow. I watched her haul a chair out of her living room. She was in her element, decorating her home for an event. But this was not just a party; this was her husband's final good-bye. I was worried about my friend.

Once all the furniture had been taken out of her living room, we placed folding chairs facing the floor-to-ceiling windows that framed her beautiful backyard. Being in the canyon, her backyard looked more like a state park, surrounded by willow and oak trees along with massive California sycamores. It was the perfect setting to celebrate John's life.

"Let's add some fresh roses to the window frames," Angel directed, pointing to a step ladder.

"Here, let me do that." I stood on the step ladder, took some roses out of a bucket, carefully staying away from the thorns, and arranged them on the valance above the windows.

"And the rest of you, place these floral arrangements around the room," she said. "I want lots of flowers."

When we were done, the velvety smell of roses engulfed the space.

Angel's friends headed home to get ready for John's funeral. I'd brought a change of clothes with me. Jack would meet me for the service.

Angel and I sat down in her kitchen for coffee. She stared out the window, choking back her emotions.

"It's okay to cry," I told her. "You taught me that."

"I know," she answered. "And believe me, I have been. One minute, I'm okay and calm, and the next, I'm hysterical. I just have to make it through this day. And I don't want to cry in front of the children."

"I understand," I said. "I can't imagine how difficult this must be for you. I'm having a hard time moving on from Jack. I thought he was the one, that we'd get married, start a family. You know, like you and John. But now, I see clearly that Jack is no John."

Mentioning his name did it. Angel cried.

"I see people moving on with their lives," she said though her tears, "you know, pumping gas, getting groceries, laughing with friends. That's when I think, *My husband is dead. How can you be happy?*"

Later that day, Jack and I took our seats for the service. I spotted Angel standing near the hall and figured she wanted to be able to make a quick getaway to her bedroom, if she needed it.

At the end of the service, Angel had disappeared. I wanted to console my friend, but by the time I made it down that long hall, a group of her other friends surrounded her.

I stood in the hall next to one of Angel's friends, who had a newborn in her arms. The baby couldn't have been more than a few days old, yet the mother was in perfect shape.

"Beautiful baby," I said. "How old?"

"Five days," she said, gently bouncing her baby boy.

"You look amazing," I said. "What's your secret?"

"I'm fostering him until I can adopt," she said. "The foster/adopt program is perfect for a single parent. Baby Lance comes with a nurse on call, and he's fully insured until he turns eighteen."

"Really? How can I find out about that?"

"Go through the county. You'll even get a small amount of money every month to help."

"Where do I sign up? I want my own baby Lance."

* * *

I did my research and found the Westside Children's Center was not far from my home, and I headed for my first meeting the following week. About twenty people from all walks of life met in a classroom.

"This class allows you to explore the foster/adopt program to find out if it's for you," a counselor said. "We provide the resources and support you need to make a difference in a child's life. Right now, we need thousands of foster homes in LA—homes for infants, siblings, older children, kids of all ethnicities and ages."

I learned that most biological parents of the foster/adopt program were addicts of some kind, their babies taken away at birth. The courts give the bio parents six months to get themselves together. During that time, volunteers like me fostered their children. If the parent didn't show the court they had changed and could properly care for their kids, the foster parent could begin the adoption process.

"Many of these children need permanent homes; they're looking for forever families."

Blondie and I were a forever family. Heck, we weren't even the same species, and I felt like she was my baby.

"We work with people from all demographic groups and backgrounds—single, married, gay, straight, people of color, white, divorced, retired, working mothers. All it takes is a commitment, and the ability to meet a child's needs. Along with kindness and compassion, and, of course, the necessary funds to care for a child. You will receive a small stipend, but this is not a money-making venture."

That's me. This felt right.

Could this program provide me with a baby, lead me to my true destiny of motherhood? Maybe I didn't need a husband after all.

28

No Love Like Dog Love

I met Angel in the parking lot at Runyon Canyon for an afternoon doggie hike, only this time, I showed up without Blondie. At the age of nineteen, Blondie was too old to hike. Heck, she had a hard time standing or walking for long periods of time. And she frequently suffered from bouts of doggie Alzheimer's where she'd sit, staring at the wall. I left her sound asleep on the bathroom tiles.

"I can't wait to tell you my good news," I told Angel in a singsong voice.

We started on the trail, Hobson and Charlie running ahead.

"I could use a little good news," she said. "Seems like I'll never get over the loss of John."

"That's understandable." I put my hand on Angel's shoulder. "But maybe this will help a little. I'm officially on the list to become a foster parent. I've completed six weeks of classes and submitted my fingerprints, and yesterday, the Los Angeles Department of Children and Family Services told me my home has been approved."

"Darling, it's really happening; you'll be a mommy soon."

My heart fluttered at the sound of her words. Adopting a baby was my calling—the reason I never had children of my own. No longer would I be the childless one among my friends. Husbandless, yes, but I would have my own baby to love, someone to raise and care for, someone who really needed me. Finally, my life made sense.

I wiped the sweat from my brow. "But first, I have to get Jack out of my apartment. That was the one stipulation of passing the home inspection. The baby has to have its own room."

"Oh, sweetikins." Angel put her arm around my shoulders. "I feel for you."

"You know, he's not a bad person," I said. "He's just a bad boyfriend."

"I really wish things had worked out between the two of you," she said as we stopped to take in the view of the Santa Monica Mountains.

I turned to her. "He doesn't know that I could have a little one in my arms any day now ... but he will soon enough. He's got to leave. I'm hoping the news might give him the kick in the pants he needs to find a new place to live."

"You've been together a while now," she said. "Must be hard for you."

"Yeah, it is, but I've got to get on with my life, and I want to raise a child and have my own family."

"And you need to prepare yourself for all that comes with motherhood"—Angel held her hands out wide and embraced me—"the good and the not so good."

We started up a steep hill, Hobson and Charlie still in the lead.

"True. The Los Angeles Department of Children and Family Services sets up foster parents for success. I'm hoping I'll be able to adopt my foster child. I just have to wait until a baby needs me." Saying these words out loud put a smile on my face. "Part of the foster adoption process includes six months of visits with the birth parents until a judge determines the future of the child."

"Even if you don't get to keep the child, at least you know you are doing something so valuable," Angel said, "giving a baby a safe space."

"So true," I answered. "And the best news is that I can do this on my own. There's a nurse on call round the clock."

"You know you can always call me too."

"That's good because I'm counting on you to be a big part of my support system."

She took my hand in hers. "Of course, darling, anything you need."

"What I need right now is strength. I'm going to talk to Jack tonight."

* * *

I came home around dinnertime to find Jack cooking. I felt anxious about breaking up. For all his faults, I loved the guy, and we had a history together—not all of it was bad. I knew him, knew what to expect, and had given up on him meeting my needs. But now, it was time to put my needs first.

The apartment smelled like Thanksgiving. I sneaked into the room, unnoticed, and watched him sing and dance while he cooked. Two years of recovery, and finally, Jack seemed to be feeling better after the accident. What a crappy time to break up.

"Smells so good in here," I said.

"Look, Susan, I'm making Blondie's favorite meal—turkey. We'll have enough left over to give it to her for months."

"I can smell that," I said. "To what do we deserve this royal treatment?"

"I want you to know how much I appreciate you."

"Really? Blondie will be so happy," I said. "Turkey and it's not even Thanksgiving."

A twinge of guilt tickled my belly. It'd been a long time since Jack made dinner for me. In fact, he hadn't helped me much since his accident.

"It's Thanksgiving, from me to you," he said with a wink. "I want to let you know how thankful I am for you. Couldn't have made it through this ordeal without your support."

Jack put down the turkey baster, grabbed me, and gave me a big, passionate kiss, the kind you felt from the top of your head to the bottom of your feet.

Now, I felt like a complete mean girl. Of course, Jack had acted selfish and self-centered; he'd been run over by a car.

"And about having a baby, I'll help you," Jack said, "the old-fashioned way, just like you want."

* * *

I wasn't sure if I felt sorry for him or guilty about planning to kick him out, but I never did talk about breaking up that day. I didn't share with Jack the good news that I could be a mommy within the next couple of months. What a complete people-pleaser.

I found out in therapy that people-pleasing could be a serious problem, learned that I confused people-pleasing with kindness. I felt responsible for how other people felt, apologized to everyone—even a lamp when I ran into it once got an apology—excessively blamed myself for everything, and basically felt apologetic for being me. I constantly filled my schedule with activities I thought other people wanted to do and had a hard time saying no. The worst part? I needed praise, craved admiration to feel good about myself.

Even in high school, friends would tell me I needed to toughen up.

"I'll give you bitch lessons," one friend had said.

Turned out, I didn't need bitch lessons. When I realized what people-pleasing did to me, I decided to do something about it.

I didn't trust that Jack had really meant what he said about being a sperm donor anyway. I didn't even know if I could get pregnant. I had already moved on from that idea. I'd tell Jack later in the week.

The next day, I could barely concentrate at work, anxious about what lay ahead. My left eyelid twitched. Could I really take care of a baby by myself? Concerns about my aging dog made matters worse. For the past month, I'd had to carry Blondie outside to use the bathroom. She didn't have the appetite she used to, and her bathroom accidents were happening several times a day.

I tried to ignore the signs, but I knew deep inside that the dreaded day I'd have to say good-bye to my four-legged baby girl was coming. I didn't know how I would live without my doggie sidekick.

I sat at my desk and buried myself with reports to take my mind off the inevitable. I always felt better when I saw a list of my accomplishments. And there were many that month. I'd gotten stories for clients in major magazines like *Condé Nast Traveler*, secured major television coverage for another client on *The Today Show*, and even got one client featured in *People Magazine*.

Jack called in a panic. "I think this is it. It's bad."

"Slow down," I said, my heart sinking. "What's bad?"

"You'd better get here right away. There's something wrong with Blondie."

I hung up the phone and ran out of the office. I drove like a madwoman, hyperventilating.

Blondie lay in the bathroom on those cool tiles, surrounded by throw-up and diarrhea.

"I found her like this," he said. I could hear the concern in his voice.

I grabbed a towel and scooped her up into my arms.

"You drive," I told Jack and kissed my dog on the top of her head.

When we arrived at the vet's office, the receptionist ushered us to the back room. Someone took Blondie from my arms and placed her in a dog crate.

"She hates crates," I said.

But she didn't seem to mind it that day. She lay down and closed her eyes.

"I love you so much," I said to her.

Blondie was the only dog in the row of empty cages. This was where pets recovered from surgery, where they waited for their owners to pick them up. Blondie had waited there many times before, but this day, my girl wouldn't be going home with me; we both knew it.

The harsh ammonia smell of the animal hospital made my stomach flip. My shoulders quaked, and my chin trembled. I yearned for the days when I'd hiked with my girl on the hills of Runyon Canyon, where she chased butterflies and sniffed the grass.

Blondie looked awful, and her breathing was labored. She managed to wag her tail and stared at me with those beautiful amber eyes like she had when I first found her in the pound.

Jack stood near her, his face wet with tears. "I didn't think I'd cry like this."

"It's okay; you love her too." I choked back my tears.

"She's not even my dog."

"I know, but you took care of her when I worked. She considered you her master when I left on business trips. Thanks for that."

Jack put his head on my shoulder and broke down.

I felt strong at that moment because I believed Blondie needed me to be. I didn't want to scare her or freak out myself.

When Dr. Winters entered the room, Jack turned his back to hide his emotion. I stood stiff, in shock. I didn't want to face this; I would rather jump out of my skin, run back in time, and take Blondie with me.

"Susan, maybe she'll rally again," the doctor said.

"I don't think so, not this time. She needs me to let go."

"Okay, we'll get the room ready," he said.

That was when I realized he looked like he might cry at any moment too.

"Can I hold her?"

"Of course."

We were rushed into another room at the hospital. A simple table in front of me was the last place Blondie would lay her head.

The vet tech brought Blondie in and placed her in my arms. I laid her on the table, facing me. She relaxed and kissed me. I breathed in her scent, wanting her sweetness to fill every fiber of my being. I rubbed my nose, my cheeks, my whole face along her back, feeling the soft down-like texture of her fur that had kept me warm on cold nights when we slept together. Nose-to-nose, I looked deep into her eyes, and she looked into mine.

One by one, the employees at the veterinarian hospital entered the room to say good-bye to her. My golden pound mutt, the one I'd rescued years before, had touched many lives.

"Good-bye, Blondie. I'll miss seeing you shake in the lobby," the receptionist said. She dried her tears, kissed her fingers, and then petted my dog.

"Blondie, such a warrior dog, she'll be missed," another employee said. She hugged me tight and left the room.

"I never thought Blondie would leave you," another employee said.

"I can't believe I'm crying so hard…." Jack held Blondie's paw in his hand.

I rested her head in my arms and said, "Oh, Blondie, you've been such a good girlie. We had quite a journey, you and me. You'll always be part of me; I'll never forget you. In heaven, you can eat as much turkey as you want. I love you so much. Look for me when it's my turn to leave this earth."

"Are you ready?" Dr. Winters said. His complexion was white.

I nodded but couldn't speak. When the tears came, dripping down my face, they landed on Blondie's golden fur.

He administered the shot. I watched Blondie's body ripple. My sweet dog's life ended.

When I let go of her, a feeling of gratitude filled my heart. Blondie had changed my life forever. She'd left me with her unconditional love.

29

Dog Love Fur-Ever

I hoped my therapist would be able to help me get through my grief. She always knew exactly what I needed to hear. Besides, sitting in my normal seat on the couch across from Beverly made me feel a tiny bit better. Even so, the moment I saw Beverly, I started to cry.

"Without Blondie, I'm lost," I said through tears. "It feels like I lost my daughter even though she was only a dog. Seems like everyone around me thinks I can easily replace her with another one. I can't."

"Of course, that's perfectly understandable," Beverly said, handing me a box of Kleenex. "It's normal to be sad, angry, or lonely for a while. What you need to concentrate on right now is going through the grieving process."

"Angel gets it; she showed up at my doorstep with flowers and took me to church, where we lit candles in Blondie's memory."

I stared at Blondie's favorite spot on the rug, the place she'd waited during my weekly sessions, now empty.

"Angel's there for you; that's good," Beverly said. "But what about Jack?"

"He's been really supportive, too, even got me a book about dealing with the loss of a dog." I placed my hand on my aching heart. "He also helped create a Blondie shrine."

"A Blondie shrine, that's nice. What's it look like?"

"I placed one of my favorite pictures of her on a small table, added her St. Francis medal, and surrounded it with candles and incense."

"Creating a shrine is an excellent way to remember and honor Blondie." Beverly looked at me lovingly. "The act of creating something beautiful like that can help heal the pain of loss."

"Speaking of loss, you know, I planned to break up with Jack right before Blondie died. Only now, he's really got to move out. Hopefully, I have a baby coming soon."

"What's your plan?"

REST AND BE THANK[...]

BLONDIE 1981-199[...]

May She Rest in Peace - Susan

Blondie memorial picture with the St. Francis charm she wore. This framed image sat in the center of my Blondie shrine (author's photograph).

"I'm clueless." I said. "But one thing I know for sure, if one more person tells me to get another dog, I'm going to explode."

"The grief from losing a pet can be as intense as the loss of any family member."

"Or more. I feel like a part of me is gone."

"Let your expressions of grief out in a healthy way. Scream as loud as you can into a pillow, hurl ice cubes against a wall, cry."

"I've cried so much that I'm surprised I have any tears left," I said, squirming in my seat. Even with my therapist, I found it hard to share my feelings without Blondie in the room. "Blondie left a huge void in my life."

"She was your best friend, your sidekick, your baby," Beverly said. "A loss like that would devastate anyone."

"It's my routine I really miss—our daily walks, her doggie greetings when I came through the door. I'm not sure who I am without her."

"Grief has a way of turning our world around to the point of being unrecognizable. In time, you'll be able to create a new routine."

"If you say so. The whole thing makes me wonder about my plans to become a parent. If I can't handle losing my dog, which I knew would happen, what if I foster a baby and have to give him or her back to drug-addicted parents? I don't think I could bear to give a child back."

Beverly leaned forward. "Don't get ahead of yourself. One day at a time, remember? You've done the work. Having your own child can be a wonderful, rewarding experience. You're moving toward your goal in an adult way."

"Maybe. But what if I'm making a mistake?"

"Stay in the moment. Right now, you need to consider the many ways you can honor Blondie and keep asking for the support you need."

I took Beverly's advice and kept my focus on the moment. But I missed Blondie so much that I thought about her at every moment; her death became my obsession. I polled coworkers about death and asked friends what they thought happened when someone died.

I'd lost my grandparents and my childhood dog, Siesta. I'd had to say good-bye to Bonnie the bunny, countless goldfish, several cats, a hamster, and even a one-eyed parakeet named Sammy Davis, Jr. But those deaths paled in comparison to the loss of Blondie.

I struggled to figure out what death meant to me. I wanted to have faith that something happened with our souls after we died. I knew Jack believed in Karma and reincarnation. He talked about his near-death experience when the car had hit him; he believed he had gone through a tunnel and toward the light but decided to stay here on Earth.

One night, while Jack watched television, I pulled out the book he had given me—*Dog Heaven* by Cynthia Rylant. The whimsical hardcover offered a peek at what heaven might look like for dogs, but it didn't do much to comfort me. I needed to know more.

"What do you think happens to the souls of dogs when they die? Can they be reincarnated too?"

"Absolutely," Jack said. "Dogs have souls like humans; they get more evolved each time they come back to Earth to burn off their Karma. Each life is an opportunity to learn the lessons they need."

"That's all very interesting," I said, taking a seat on the couch next to him and putting my feet up on the coffee table, "but I don't want to learn the details of reincarnation. I want to know when my dog will come back and where I can find her."

"That's not how it works," Jack said, shaking his head. "Reincarnation is a great mystery. I've read that the reason dogs travel in packs is because they have as much of an individual soul as they do group soul, both equally important. Dogs operate on a group level as well as an individual one. Does that make sense?"

"No, it doesn't. All I want to know is what I need to do to be reunited with Blondie."

"You're joking, right?"

"No, I'm not. I need to find her. Life's so incredibly unfair. Why did God give me Blondie to love and only allow her to live such a short time?"

"Nineteen years is not a short life, Susan, especially for a dog."

"It is for me."

* * *

The next day, when I had trouble concentrating at work again, I went outside to breathe in some fresh air. Fresh air always made me feel better but not this time.

I noticed a woman with her puppy struggling at the end of a leash. The puppy pulled, jumped, tried to run, but the leash held it back. The puppy's tan color reminded me of Blondie's, and his ears perked up like hers too. When the woman and her puppy got close enough, I noticed those amber eyes.

"Excuse me." I stopped the woman and her puppy. "That's a beautiful puppy."

I looked into the puppy's eyes, searching for Blondie. The young dog squirmed and cried, not wanting to stop for anything, especially for the crazy lady staring at him like a madwoman.

I asked him silently, *Are you my dog?*

"Oh, thanks," the woman replied. "She's six months old. Quite a handful. She doesn't like the leash."

They walked away, leaving me there on the sidewalk, shattered.

I didn't know what I would have done anyway if the dog had answered, *Yes, I'm Blondie reincarnated, but I have a new owner in this life. Sorry.*

The following week, I headed back to the vet's office to pick up Blondie's ashes. I sat in the waiting room where I'd always needed to console a frightened Blondie. That day, my lap remained empty.

I recognized actress Suzanne Pleshette in the waiting room. On her lap was a cute little dachshund. I took a seat next to her, remembering the '70s sitcom she'd starred in—*The Bob Newhart Show*. I had grown up watching her on television, so I felt like I knew her, but I didn't.

I'd seen many celebrities in that waiting room before, but I always kept my cool. I got a thrill when I recognized Mike Myers, James Woods, and even Jack Lemmon with his human-like black standard poodle. But not even a star encounter could brighten my dark mood.

"This dog's costing me a fortune," Suzanne said to no one in particular.

I looked at her. "They're worth every penny."

"You don't have an ornery dachshund like this, do you?" She held out her dog, who was wiggling and squirming in her arms.

I didn't have an ornery anything. I tried to hold back my tears. Didn't want to fall apart in front of the famous actress. But my plan didn't work.

"Sorry ... I ... lost ... my ... dog...."

"Oh dear, you don't need to be sorry," she said. "I know how difficult it is to lose someone you love. I'm the one who's sorry. Here's a dog hug." She lifted her dog toward me and said to her dachshund, "Give this sad lady a kiss; she lost her dog, so be nice."

He licked my face as if to say everything was going to be all right.

After she left, I sat by myself and waited, depressed to the core. I closed my eyes and tried to picture Blondie there with me but couldn't. I attempted to visualize her running to me in a field of flowers. No use, as I couldn't picture her at all. My mind was blank, frozen, numb.

"Susan.... Susan.... Susan?" the receptionist said.

I looked up, embarrassed. I'd zoned out.

"Here you go." She handed me a plain gold canister filled with my dog's ashes.

"That's it?"

I took it from her and walked like a robot to my car. It didn't feel right to be leaving my vet without a leash in my hand, only a small, round golden canister. I stood outside for a moment and stared at it. Time to face facts. Blondie was gone, and she wouldn't be coming back.

30

Fluff Ball Needs a Home

With a foster baby on the horizon, the thought of adopting a dog seemed ridiculous. But the truth was, I still craved unconditional love in my life. That was when I considered volunteering at a local animal shelter, so I could get my fix every day by walking dogs while making a difference for homeless pets. The perfect solution was waiting for me at the Lange Foundation, a rescue organization that was located right around the corner. A quick phone call to introduce myself, and I headed right over.

On the short car ride to the foundation, I realized that volunteering made sense. I'd learned though therapy that I was drawn to helping others who, like me, needed love, whether they be human or canine.

You'd never know there was an animal shelter located inside the nondescript building. I wondered if I was even in the right place until I saw a big dog paw on the sign. A big black cat greeted me when I entered.

"Hello there," I said to the cat and bent down to pet him.

"You're the one who lost your dog, right?" a young woman who worked there said. "I'm Marie."

"Yes, that's me," I said. "I'm here to help."

"Let's get you started," Marie said. "Follow me."

We walked toward the back of the building where dogs were waiting in large runs for their forever homes. The place smelled clean—unlike the shelter where I'd rescued Blondie—but the sound was the same—desperate dogs barking for love. I wanted to take them all home.

In one run, I saw a dog that resembled Blondie—same size, color, and amber eyes. My heart melted. She wagged her tail when I passed by. Maybe I needed to reconsider my resolve not to get a dog.

Marie nodded to a miniature pinscher that looked thin and malnourished and said, "He's in quarantine until he gets some meat on those bones."

But by far, the biggest racket came from a puppy at the end of the row of runs.

"Satin, it's okay," Marie said. She turned to me. "He's our new puppy."

The little black ball of fluff cried and clawed at his cage, bouncing off the walls to get my attention. I couldn't tell his tail from his head until I saw his bright white baby teeth and pink tongue. He looked like a Muppet. I had to touch him and make sure he was real.

"Can I walk him?"

"No," Marie said. "He's too young to take outside, because he hasn't had all his shots."

She tried to calm him down, but the little pup carried on.

I was dying to wrap my arms around him. "Can I at least hold him?" I asked.

"Sure. Looks like he won't quiet down until you do."

Marie opened the cage and the floppy mop of a dog barreled out to me.

"Wow, he really likes you," she said.

Baldwin poses for a picture. Who says black dogs aren't photogenic? (photograph by Pam Marks, PawPrince Studios).

I bent down and allowed his pink tongue to bathe my face with sweet kisses. He made me laugh for the first time since I'd lost Blondie.

"You're so cute!" I picked him up and rocked him back and forth like a baby until he settled in my arms.

"His name is Satin," she said.

"What kind of dog is Satin?" I asked.

He sighed and closed his eyes.

"We think he's a poodle mix."

Owning a poodle had never entered my mind, but this little guy sure was a cutie.

"Where did he come from?" I sat down on the concrete floor, stroking him to sleep.

"We got him out of the Burbank pound," Marie said. "We don't have his backstory."

"I'm sure he'll find the perfect home," I said.

Satin opened his eyes and began bathing me in kisses again.

"Here, let's put him back."

Reluctantly, I handed him back to Marie. When she placed him back in the run, he cried like a banshee. My heart did flip-flops. Marie handed me a leash, and we headed back to the Blondie look-alike.

"Why don't you take Sheba out?" She opened the cage, and the little blonde dog stepped out, ready.

As I exited the building with the Blondie lookalike, Satin's cries tugged at my heart.

* * *

The next day, I spent my lunch break at the Lange Foundation. I couldn't wait to see Satin again. He must have sensed my presence because the moment the front door closed behind me, I recognized his howls.

I hurried to get to him, his barks calling to me. He saw me and then ran to the gate of his dog run. When I opened it, Satin snagged the pants of my new DKNY suit, but I didn't care. Dog love was worth all my expensive suits.

I inhaled his sweet puppy smell that reminded me of sunshine and happiness. He bathed my face with kisses again. Then he curled up and snuggled in my lap.

"Oh no, I'm a goner."

I returned to the office but couldn't stop thinking about Satin. Should I bring him home? I called my mom, knowing she'd be the voice of reason.

"Mom, I saw this little black puppy at the Lange Foundation today," I told her. "You don't think I should get another dog, do you?"

"You're a dog person," she said. "Of course, you should get another dog."

"What about the foster baby?"

"What about it?" Mom said. "You've been around dogs all your life. I'm sure your baby will too."

She had a point, but still, her answer came as a surprise. I had been certain Mom would lecture me on the responsibilities of a baby and tell me to wait.

I'm Not Single, I Have a Dog

My relationship with Mom seemed to be changing. With the help of my therapist, Beverly, I'd learned how to let Mom's insults and passive-aggressive comments go. I felt like Mom's answer proved that my resolve to get close to her was working. She finally recognized me for myself, not for the daughter she wanted me to be.

I called Angel next to get her opinion.

"I've fallen in love with a little black dog; he's up for adoption, but I'm not sure I'm ready. What do you think?"

"Darling, are we ever ready for what lies ahead?" my wise friend counseled. "Go for the love."

The blessing from Angel carried a lot of weight, but I still felt torn about the decision. Blondie's death had left me traumatized. I didn't know if I could go through that again.

That was when Mom called back.

"Go get your dog," she said. "I bought him for you."

"Really?"

"Yes, really," she said.

"But how'd you know where he was?"

Satin (Baldwin) and I pose for a picture with our messy hair (photograph by Jim Crawford).

"You mentioned the Lange Foundation when you called to ask me about him."

"That's about the nicest thing anyone has ever done for me," I said.

"I hoped that instead of focusing on losing Blondie you could celebrate the years of joy she brought into your life with this new dog."

"Oh, Mom." I put my hand on my heart. "I am so grateful."

"Stop thanking me and go get your dog," she said.

After hanging up the phone, I ran out of the office to pick up my new dog.

Little Satin waited for me behind the front desk. When he saw me, he wagged his little stump of a tail, and his entire body gyrated. He had known we were meant to be together the moment he saw me. I knew too. I picked him up and hugged him tight.

"You are something else, mister."

He nudged my nose and made me laugh.

That little black dog became a symbol of my mother's acceptance of me, the real me. I believe she'd bought him for me, knowing that he could give me unconditional love.

I didn't warn Jack about my new dog. Why would I? I didn't need his approval. He'd stopped trying to make a baby with me, just as I'd suspected he would. His bad habit of not coming though with his promises made me glad I'd stayed on course with the foster/adopt program.

"Isn't he adorable?"

"What?" Jack said. "Tell me that's not yours."

Satin ran up to him as if to say, *I'm here! Don't you love me?* He sniffed around his new home.

"Jack, meet Satin, my new dog."

"I can't believe you got another dog," Jack said. "You're not over Blondie yet."

"This little guy will help me get through my grief," I said.

This time I was prepared for a dog. I got Blondie's dog food and water bowls out of the cupboard and placed them on the floor. I'd almost gotten rid of them after Blondie died, but something had told me to wait. I was glad I'd listened to my inner voice.

Jack leaned against the kitchen counter, arms crossed. "Well, I'm not going to take care of him like I did Blondie."

"I know," I said, "and I wouldn't ask you to."

"Look, it's either me or the dog."

"Really?" I stated, my hands on my hips. "This little guy is not going anywhere. Anyway, I've been meaning to talk to you about our living arrangement."

"Yeah, me too," Jack said.

Satin nudged my ankle, and I picked him up and looked directly at Jack. "We haven't really been a couple for some time now," I said. "We sleep in separate rooms and don't even like to do the same things."

"I told you, I need to check out live music as often as possible," he said. "It's in my blood."

"I know it is, and I'd never ask you to change. But I don't want to change either. I finished those adoption classes and could have a baby any day now."

"What the fuck?" He pushed off the counter and paced back and forth. "I don't want a baby."

"I know you don't. That's why you need to move out. I've been paying the rent and bills myself since your accident, and I'm done. I'm going to need your room for the baby."

"That's it," he said. "I don't want to live someplace I'm not wanted."

"Jack, it's not like that."

"What do you mean? You just kicked me out for a dog and a baby."

"I think it will be better for both of us to go our own ways."

"I'm out of here," he said.

Jack packed up his stuff and left that night. His actions didn't surprise me much. It was time for both of us to move on. Still, I felt a deep sense of loss. But my new fluff ball (and my therapist) helped me work through it.

Once again, a dog had helped me find my way out of a relationship mess. Little did I know that the little dog would do more than that; he'd open a whole new world to me filled with dog love.

31

A Good Dog Is a Tired Dog

"Your name's not Satin," I told the little black ball of fluff.

He sat next to me while I caught the middle of the movie *Clueless*. When the main character and her trendy friends referred to cute boys as Baldwins, I realized that was this little dog's name.

"Baldwin," I announced.

Mr. Fluff turned to me and jumped into my lap.

"And you're not a poodle either," I told him. "Dr. Winters says you're a Puli—whatever that is. It doesn't matter. I love you, no matter what."

I couldn't wait for Angel, Hobson, and the gang to meet my new dog. We showed up at her home that very evening.

"Darling, let me see this precious boy," Angel said as she opened the front door.

Baldwin didn't hesitate; he darted inside and ran laps around Hobson, making us all dizzy. The elder Scottie dog rolled around with my puppy until Baldwin went wild with the "zoomies," running around in circles, completely oblivious of his surroundings. I worried that he'd break something but had a hard time catching him.

One moment, he played nice, and the next, he raced around Angel's house, low to the ground, his butt tucked underneath him as if herding invisible sheep.

"Easy, Baldwin," I said, hoping to slow him down before he hurt himself or broke one of Angel's expensive treasures.

He stopped for a moment and then broke into a flat-out gallop again. I grabbed him before he slammed into Hobson.

"I've never had a dog like this," I said. "He's a handful; he wants to play all the time. If I'm not throwing the ball for him, I'm running him around the block ... several blocks."

"I can see that, darling," Angel said. "What kind of dog is he?"

"My vet says he's a Puli, a Hungarian sheepdog. Apparently, that means he's super smart. Doc says I have to train him. The smarter the dog, the more training they require. Training keeps them from acting out their destructive behaviors."

"I know an amazing dog trainer in Beverly Hills—Shelby Marlow," Angel told me. Of course, she did. Angel knew everyone in town.

"I've never had luck with training dogs. Didn't have to do anything with Blondie, except love her. This guy's a whole different story. I'd better get her number."

"Everyone goes to her, even Oprah." Angel took Baldwin from me. "You need to learn some manners, don't you, little man?"

"He needs more than manners," I watched as he almost crashed into a side table.

"I love the dreadlocks and that face," Angel said. "He looks almost human or like a Muppet."

"That's exactly what I thought. He looks kinda like Cookie Monster."

"I see the resemblance," Angel sat down on the living room couch and motioned for me to join her.

"He's a big baby, and he wakes me up at five in the morning. I'm so sleep-deprived...." I closed my eyes for emphasis.

"Brilliant! You'll be ready for your adopted child. Sleep deprivation's a sign of motherhood. When will you bring a child home?"

"Soon. I'm on a list to foster a newborn. Can't wait till I get the call."

* * *

Before I began a six-week puppy class, I bought the book *How to Raise and Train a Puli* by Ellanor H. Anderson. I learned that the Pulik—yes, the plural of Puli was Pulik—was an ancient herding breed, raised to herd sheep and cattle. In their native Hungary, Pulik still helped ranchers with their flocks. Dogs from the herding group needed a job to keep their minds stimulated, their bodies moving. I'd explore that in training.

We met the following Saturday morning at a nearby parking lot. Ten people and their puppies gathered around trainer Shelby Marlow.

"Group classes like this are the perfect way to help your puppy learn the basics of obedience," Shelby said. She looked more like a blonde talk-show host than a dog trainer. "This is the opportunity to socialize your puppy, one of the most important aspects of training."

There were all sorts of dogs in class, and Baldwin wanted to rile them up. To him, class at the park meant play time, and he didn't want to slow down to learn.

"Settle, mister," I said.

Baldwin during his first obedience class in Beverly Hills. He came in first place! (photograph by the late Dan Del Campos).

Baldwin didn't listen to me; instead, he pulled the leash out of my hand and ran toward his new bestie—a shaggy, long-haired bearded collie. Beardy's owner, a skinny guy, about my age, was wearing a base ball cap, khaki shorts, a wrinkled tee, and ... a wedding ring. This time I checked right away.

"Your dog is adorable," I said. "Male or female?"

"Male. Aren't you, buddy?" the skinny guy said, turning to his hairy sidekick.

I bent down to pet his dog, and Baldwin took the opportunity to take off.

"Don't chase him," Shelby yelled to me. "If you chase him, he'll think it's a game."

I found it difficult not to run after my dog, but I listened to the trainer. Instead, I turned and pretended to run the other way like she told me. It worked! Baldwin wove in and out of the students and their dogs as fast as he could to catch me.

"Good boy, Baldwin," I exclaimed.

This trainer really knew her stuff.

"Is your dog an aspiring actor?" the dog owner next to me asked.

"What do you mean?"

"That's Greg Kinnear."

Turned out, I'd been chatting with actor Greg Kinnear the whole time. Maybe I could actually train Baldwin to be a dog star. I accidently dropped Baldwin's leash, imagining his name on the credits of a movie. He took off again.

Shelby stepped on Baldwin's leash when he sprinted by, jerking him to a stop.

"You've got to keep hold of your dog's leash," she said. "Keep his attention on you through training. Let's start with a simple sit."

As directed by Shelby, I held the treat above Baldwin's nose, and to my surprise, he sat right away. It was as if he'd been waiting for me to train him all along.

I patted him. "Good sit, boy."

Next, I taught Baldwin to shake. I bent down, a treat in one hand, holding out my other for his paw. He looked into my eyes. I saw him think about it and then lift his paw to place it in my hand.

"Good boy, Baldwin. Shake."

Never before had I trained a dog to do anything more than sit. And even that was iffy.

Baldwin takes a jump at an agility trial. He came in first place! (photograph by Pam Marks, PawPrince Studios).

31. A Good Dog Is a Tired Dog

Baldwin turned out to be the class superstar, especially when it came to the dog agility equipment Shelby set up.

"Agility helps puppies build self-esteem."

While other dogs were too frightened to walk over a wobbly bridge Shelby set up, Baldwin showed no fear. He didn't have a problem sailing over the jumps, either. Maybe agility could be his job. I didn't have a clue about agility training. I'd had no idea that dog sports would soon become the center of my life.

* * *

My work schedule got crazy busy again. Every client wanted me to organize a press trip, which meant leaving my new puppy behind. I hated to travel, especially since I didn't have Jack living with me to take over chores. I missed having a man at home to help me, but I also appreciated my own independence.

"There's got to be a solution that doesn't include inviting an unhealthy man to live with me."

Sure enough, I found a brand-new doggie daycare and boarding facility nearby, where I could leave Baldwin. I tried the daycare to see if he liked it and surprised myself when I broke into tears at the thought of leaving my new baby in a strange place.

"I can't believe I'm crying," I said.

"Lots of pet parents cry, just like moms do on the first day of kindergarten," the owner of the facility said.

I dried my tears and watched Baldwin walk with his head held high right into the middle of the pack.

"That's my boy."

* * *

Mom loved the little dog she bought me. And my black fluff ball loved the house on Dearborn Street, which had the perfect yard for him to run.

"He's so cute," Mom said.

Baldwin and I followed her into their bedroom.

"And smart," I added. "He got first place in his puppy class."

Baldwin sat by my side as I spoke. Mom bent down to pet him.

"He's so soft," she commented.

"And he doesn't shed either," I said proudly.

"Where's Jack?" Mom asked.

"We broke up," I answered trying again to push down my emotions.

That was when the reality of our breakup hit me. Jack would not be my husband. We would not have a family together. Why did my wall of denial begin to crumble at that moment in front of Mom? I couldn't express my feelings in front of her. Instead, I bit my lower lip to keep from crying. Mom hated it when I cried.

"Help me change the sheets on your dad's bed."

"What do you mean, Dad's bed?" I said. "It's your bed too."

"Not anymore. I've been sleeping on the couch. He doesn't sleep very well, and he wakes up a million times a night. He's convinced there are squirrels in the bed."

"What are you talking about, Mom? He's seeing squirrels?"

"Squirrels or spiders. He screams at me to get them out of the bed."

"He screams at you?"

"That's not all," she said. "He can't walk any longer, and that damn wheelchair is killing me. It's so heavy; I can barely get it in and out of the car."

"I had no idea things had gotten that bad," I said, concentrating on not freaking out in front of her.

Dad still looked and sounded like the man who'd raised me, the man I admired. He had no problem recognizing me. Still, Mom's latest news made my heart sink to my toes.

"Mom, you need help."

"No, no, I can take care of him myself," Mom said. She laid a set of clean sheets on the dresser. "You've been through enough, losing your dog, breaking it off with Jack. I know how you feel."

"You do?" *Was Mom actually trying to comfort me?* I couldn't hold back my tears any longer.

"Listen, before I met your father, I had this boyfriend. I've wanted to tell you kids about him for a long time, but your father told me not to."

She ignored my tears, placing a plastic bed liner on the bed. Mom motioned for me to move to the other side of the bed. I wiped my face and tried to pull myself together.

"Here, help me with this."

We smoothed the liner over the bed, tightening the corners.

"He can't control himself; he goes to the bathroom in bed most nights. And guess who has to clean up that mess?"

"Mom, this is serious. Why didn't you tell me things were this bad?"

Tears ran down my cheeks. Now, my heart ached not only for me, but for Dad and Mom too.

"The boy I dated before your father..."

31. A Good Dog Is a Tired Dog

"I want to hear what you have to say, but can we discuss your past relationship tomorrow?" I managed to get my words out through my tears. "I can't process another detail tonight." Mom didn't even try to change my mind.

My brain felt like it would explode, and I couldn't handle anything more than my latest break-up and the realization that Dad's health issues were way more serious than I had thought. I needed a moment to collect my thoughts before I heard about Mom's past, the big family secret.

"You'll be okay," Mom surprised me with her caring words.

We finished making the bed in silence. After we were done, I grabbed Baldwin, said my good-byes, and left.

On the drive home, I thought about how strange it was that, after all these years, Mom had picked that night to open up and share her big secret with me. We Hartzler kids knew Mom hid something about her past but understood never to ask about it.

I planned to get back to our conversation. I couldn't imagine what she'd reveal about the guy she'd dated before she met Dad. I'd call her for the details first thing in the morning.

32

A Sad Tale

The next morning, my phone woke me from a deep sleep. Instead of answering, I yelled to no one in particular, "Go away."

I turned over, ignored the persistent ringing, and did my best to slip back into the final minutes of my dream where Blondie ran through a field of flowers, her blonde fur blowing in the wind. The dream seemed real, but no sooner had the ringing stopped than it began again.

"All right," I said and got my butt out of bed to grab my phone.

Before I could even say hello, Will said, "Sue, are you sitting down?" He had a tone that could only mean bad news, the worst kind of news.

My stomach dropped and I answered, "Dad died."

"No, Sue, Mom died."

Did I hear him right? Did he say Mom died? He didn't make sense. Dad was the one who had been sick for so long. "You mean Dad, right?"

He sighed. "No, I mean Mom. Dad called me this morning. Somehow, he'd gotten himself out of bed and found Mom on the couch. I'm here now. I've called the mortuary."

I dropped the phone and heard myself make a deep, guttural sound, a cry that came from my soul, maybe from another time, and it hurt like hell.

"Not Mommy, not Mommy." I fell to the floor, curled into a fetal position, and sobbed.

Mom is dead?

My brother's words broke me, split me in two. I floated above my body. I witnessed myself fall apart, watched as another Susan cried out in pain. This couldn't be me. Then I remembered Mom's secret. She was about to expose whatever it was she had kept hidden from us for so long; she couldn't die now. *How would I live without her, without knowing her secret?* Our relationship had finally been in a good place, only to be taken away.

I shoved on a pair of shoes and a jacket, grabbed my purse, keys,

Baby Baldwin gives me a big kiss (photograph by the late Dan Del Campos).

and my dog and ran outside to my car. I had to see Mom for myself, to tell her I loved her one last time in the family home where I'd lived since age four. The place that held so many memories. Baldwin sat in my lap while I drove, trying his best to cheer me up.

"Stop licking my face, boy," I said. "I can't see through my tears already. Don't need your tongue in the way too."

Like Mom, Baldwin hated to see me cry. But he was super smart. The black ball of fluff seemed to understand what I'd said and stopped kissing me. He curled up and snuggled next to me instead.

When we arrived at the family home, the first thing I noticed was crows covering our yard. The full half-acre, both front and back, looked like a sea of black feathers. The birds weren't on other lawns in the neighborhood, just ours, and Baldwin stayed by my side; he didn't even jump out of the car to chase them.

Mom lay motionless on the sofa in that dark, dingy den. The family room where we had eaten dinner together on TV trays was her final resting place.

Mom wore her favorite pink-flowered muumuu. Dad sat in front of her, his hands shaking. Will was on the phone in the kitchen.

"Your mom, my love, my best friend," Dad said. "What's going to happen to me now?"

"Don't worry, Dad," I said. "We'll figure something out. You're not alone."

With Mom gone, the extent of Dad's disease could no longer be covered up.

As soon as Will finished his call, he joined us in the den. He looked pale, broken, traumatized. "Erin's flying in next week," he said. "I called the church. We'll have to plan a service."

Everything seemed fine as long as we discussed business, even if that business surrounded Mom's death.

"I can write her obit for the paper," I said.

All I wanted to do was sleep, be unconscious, dream of a better time when we all played our part of a loving family.

In public, I acted like I had it all together. No one knew that after Mom died, I went into a downhill spiral so deep that I thought I would never be able to crawl out. Deep inside, the idea of life without Mom crushed me. I cried myself to sleep, trying to process the reality.

* * *

Although I was no longer seeing my therapist weekly, Beverly told me her door was always open, and I couldn't wait to get back to her office. That little bungalow had become my safe place.

I sat down in my usual spot, and this time, Baldwin curled up in the same exact spot Blondie used to sit.

"I feel lost in the world," I said to Beverly. My voice wavered. "In a weird way, Mom anchored me. I don't know what I'll do without her."

"Saying good-bye to a parent is one of the hardest things to face," Beverly told me, "especially when it's sudden, like the loss of your mom."

"Angel was out of town when it happened." I ran my hands down my thighs. "She's been spending time in Jamaica without a phone or email. But she called me the night Mom died and came back to help me through this. She was the first person to show up at my family's church for the funeral service."

Beverly raised her eyebrows. "Did Angel know your mother?"

"No, they never met, but she was there for me. Baldwin's been there for me too."

"I'm sure they're both a comfort."

"Thank God for them." Tears brimmed in my eyes. "I can't turn to Dad for help. Parkinson's has taken a toll on him; the medications make him hallucinate. He can't walk, and he's depressed about the loss of his wife. They were married for forty-six years. He's so fragile. I feel more like his parent now."

Beverly handed me a box of Kleenex. "It's hard to parent your father," she said. "When you were young, he was the person you turned to for guidance, for protection."

"The man who raised me is not there anymore. I feel like an orphan now. The least I can do for both Mom and Dad is to move home and supervise his care. Will, Erin, and I are all in agreement."

"When one sibling shoulders most of the burden of Mom or Dad's care, it can create resentment," Beverly said. "Not only for the person who takes on the responsibility, but also for the siblings who don't."

I patted Baldwin. "The three of us discussed everything and came up with the solution. I'm going to take care of Dad, and my brother will handle the money. Erin's busy with her family, but she'll be there for back-up."

"You still might want to consider discussing the situation with a neutral third-party to avoid potential problems down the line." Beverly's fingers formed a steeple.

"I thought she'd live forever," I said, wiping my eyes. "At least she died peacefully in her sleep."

"What a blessing. Isn't that how everyone would like to go?" Beverly sat back in her chair. "But a sudden death is harder on those left behind."

"I can't believe all the lives she touched. More than a hundred people came to her service, even in the rain on Super Bowl Sunday." I sat up straight, gathered all the used tissues, and wadded them into a ball. "Her students, adults now, shared how Mom had made them want to learn. The mailman came, her dry cleaner too, and clerks from the grocery store and Macy's. It felt strange to hear other people describe her in ways I hadn't known about. Like the fact that she wrote poetry. Who knew?"

"The realization that she had another life, a life that had nothing to do with you, can be strange," Beverly said, "but it's impossible to know everything about another person."

"She didn't know everything about me, either. Mom never met Angel personally. But she would've loved that a celebrity came to her funeral."

"Tell her now. Death does not mean the end. Nothing says you can't maintain a relationship with your mother beyond the grave. Your conversations can continue."

"She'll never see me get married"—my chest ached—"never meet the child I'm going to adopt. I need my mommy. Now, she's gone."

"A parent's death can bring on regrets," Beverly said, looking at me with her kind eyes.

"I'm filled with regrets and frustration because Mom wanted to tell me a secret the night she died. I missed my chance. Now, she's gone, and I'll never know."

"What do you mean?" Beverly asked.

"The night she died, Mom was about to share some big secret with me. She said she'd discussed telling us kids about something with Dad, but he told her not to. That night, I learned how serious my dad's illness was. On top of that, the realization of my break-up with Jack hit me ... hard. I told Mom I couldn't take in another issue. I wanted to be present when she shared her big secret. Now, I'll never know."

"Don't blame yourself," Beverly said, her forehead creased. "She'd had forty-two years to tell you. You only had one night."

* * *

A week later, I woke and remembered something Mom had told me before she died. I called Will to tell him without considering any potential consequences.

"Do you have a copy of Mom and Dad's will?" I asked, wiping the sleep from my eyes.

"It's in a safe deposit box at the bank," he answered. "Why?"

"Mom told me she and Dad were leaving the house to me."

"What?" Will's voice became shrill. "They'd never do that. They'd split everything evenly between the three of us."

I shook my head in disbelief. "Ask Dad, and he'll tell you."

"I don't have to ask anyone," Will shouted. "She'd never leave the family home to you. Is that why you moved back?"

"No," I said, now fully awake. "I moved home because I wanted to help."

"You can't steal the house, Sue."

"I'm not trying to steal anything. All I asked is to see the will. It's my right."

"Your right? What about me and Erin? We have rights too."

Will never did show me the will, but I found out that my parents never got around to making any changes. As Will had predicted, everything was split evenly. My siblings thought I'd lied. My innocent question had caused even more grief.

32. A Sad Tale

With Mom's passing, my family unraveled before my eyes. Will, Erin, and I were not the loving and supportive siblings I'd once believed we were. We acted more like strangers than family. If not for friends like Angel and the unconditional love of my little black dog, Baldwin, I didn't know what I would've done.

The next day, I got a call from the Westside Children's Center.

"We have a newborn baby for you to foster."

33

Pick of the Litter

I held the phone in my hand and allowed myself to enjoy the good news for a change. I'd wanted this baby for so long, but sadly, my joy was momentary.

"How perfect! I moved to a house in the Valley. It has a yard."

"I'm sure it's a wonderful place," she said, "but unfortunately, you're registered as being a resident of West Los Angeles, and by moving to the Valley, it's impossible to be a part of the foster/adopt program with the Westside Children's Center."

I hadn't considered this when I moved in with Dad.

My heart ached, and I said through tears, "But I still want a baby."

"I understand, and I'm sorry; however, we work under strict guidelines. You need to begin the process again at a facility near your new home."

Learning that I couldn't bring this baby who needed me into my life felt like another blow. The news brought back my abortion. I drew my knees to my chest and rocked back and forth, wondering if this was a sign that I needed to give up my dream. I didn't know how long I'd been sitting at the kitchen table like that, but I was awakened by the phone.

"Darling, it's fabulous here," Angel said. She was now living at Cape Cod with her Jamaican boyfriend.

Friends like Angel moved on in their lives. Me? I felt stuck. My depression was so bad that I could hardly get out of bed. Deep inside, anger over the loss of Mom left me exhausted. On top of that, Will and Erin treated me like shit, acted like I'd moved home to rob them of their inheritance. Maybe not the best environment to bring a baby to anyway. I felt miserable but thrilled for Angel. She'd found a new love.

"I'm so happy you found a new man. You deserve love," I said.

"You deserve love too," Angel said. "What's wrong?"

33. *Pick of the Litter*

"How'd you know something was wrong?" I asked.

"I know you, darling."

"I got the call about a newborn, but since I've moved to the Valley, I am no longer in the district of the center. I have to begin the whole process over."

"You must start over? A baby ... that's your dream."

Her words made me break down in tears.

"How can I care for a baby? Caring for Dad is a full-time job."

"You are so strong. Look at everything you've been though."

"I don't know," I said, blowing my nose. "I worry about bringing a baby here. Dad's got dementia from his Parkinson's. He knows who I am most of the time but rarely makes sense when trying to communicate."

"Oh, darling, that *is* sad news. Maybe you could take some time off and join me in Jamaica. It's a magical place."

"I'd love to. A trip would give me something to look forward to. Maybe for Thanksgiving. I'll see if my brother or sister can take my place and give me a little break."

*   *   *

It took two people to care for Dad. His full-time caretaker—Jesse, from the Philippines—lifted him in and out of his wheelchair, dressed him, helped him bathe, took him to the bathroom. Jesse also cooked and cleaned. When he wasn't doing something for Dad, Jesse spent time in the garage, smoking cigarettes. I thought about getting someone else, but Dad liked him. Besides, we paid him directly so the price was better than it would have been if we went though an agency. It would be difficult to find someone new who Dad liked.

My duties included keeping track of Dad's medications, driving him to various doctor appointments, grocery shopping, and managing the house. I also tried to keep Dad's mind engaged by taking him to classes, grief groups, anything I thought would help. He acted more like a three-year-old than a father.

Overseeing Dad's care monopolized my waking hours, but I liked it. Dad needed me.

"I want to go home," Dad said one evening.

He was already sitting in the den, watching CNN. My first instinct was to offer comfort.

I said, "Daddy, look around you. You *are* home; you're sitting in your red chair."

"No, I'm not!" he yelled. "I want to go home ... now."

"Dad, listen—"

"No, you listen," he said, shuffling to his feet. "I want to go home; that's final. Hear me?"

I nodded. "Okay."

I called Jesse to bring his walker, sent the two of them out the front door, and welcomed Dad home at the back door.

"You're back," I said. "Did you have a nice time?"

"Yes, I had lunch with Hillary Clinton."

Turned out, CNN had aired an interview with the former first lady that afternoon. I felt happy when Dad had pleasant hallucinations, but I missed the man I called Daddy, the man who'd raised me.

* * *

The family home flooded me with childhood memories. I hadn't lived there for more than twenty years and rarely, if ever, spent the night.

From a young age, I'd loved to rifle through the bottom drawer of Mom's dresser and uncover treasures from the past. I'd spend hours sitting Indian-style, examining the collection of old family photos with Siesta snuggled beside me.

Mom had liked it when I showed interest in my heritage. She'd watch me take everything out, surround myself with childhood photos of her and her brothers, aunts, uncles, and grandparents—most of whom, I'd never met.

"Who's this?" I asked her, holding an old black-and-white portrait of a couple printed on extra-thick paper like they did in the late 1800s.

"That's my grandmother, Sadie, and my grandpa, Robert—your great-grandparents," Mom said. "You remind me of Sadie. A strong woman who ran the family farm in Quebec. Not much Sadie couldn't do, just like you."

The memory made me smile. I hadn't looked in Mom's drawer in years. I couldn't wait to see all the old, familiar faces immortalized in photos.

I sat Indian-style again and opened the drawer to the past with Baldwin snuggled next to me, just like Siesta used to.

"Good boy, Baldwin."

He sighed, closed his eyes, and fell asleep. I appreciated the respite from his puppy-ness.

I expected to see Sadie and the gang, all the old family photos, but they weren't there. Instead, they were replaced by envelopes, papers, and photos I later realized were from *my childhood*.

33. Pick of the Litter

A plain white envelope sat on top. Mom's perfect handwriting spelled out my name, the capital S curved so that it looked like a work of art.

"*Susan's first tooth,*" I read aloud, peeked inside, and found a single tiny white baby tooth.

Mom had kept it safe all these years.

"Look at this, Bozzie Bear."

Baldwin raised his head to sniff my baby tooth and then curled up to sleep again.

"That's weird.... I wonder why Mom never showed this to me."

Another envelope fell to my lap.

"Susan's first haircut." A lock of my white-blonde hair tied with a pink ribbon had been carefully placed inside. "I had no idea she'd kept all this stuff."

Next, my baby announcement. It reminded me of the story Mom had loved to tell about how she'd taped bows to my bald head, so everyone would know she had a girl.

The picture of me from grad night at Disneyland in 1976, where I wore a white pantsuit with my low-rider bell-bottoms and a tight button-down plaid blouse under a matching vest. Mom had taken me shopping for that outfit.

Baldwin yawned, stretched, and fell back asleep.

A stack of my report cards sat on top of so many pictures of me. There was me as a toddler, me in grade school, high school, at the prom. I uncovered announcements sent to Mom when I made the dean's list in junior high and again in college.

"It's all me. Everything in this drawer is me."

I looked at Baldwin, sleeping by my side, and couldn't hold back my tears.

"She did this. She moved the old photos and replaced them with my history."

All the painful memories of her faded away.

"Mom knew I'd come here."

The resentments I'd carried for so long disappeared. I'd found the proof of Mom's true feelings for her youngest daughter. She loved me.

I imagined Mom reaching out to do something I'd craved from her my entire life—cradle me in her arms, rock me back and forth, let me cry. I saw myself as a child, sitting at her side, my arms wrapped around her leg, my head in her lap. She stroked my hair and leaned as close as possible to whisper in my ear like mothers do.

"There, there, baby girl. I'm here for you. I love you, no matter what, and everything's going to be all right."

For the first time in my life, I understood the complication of my mother's love for me.

And for the first time in Baldwin's puppy life, he didn't lick my tears away. Instead, he crawled onto my lap and waited while I cried.

34

Learning to Weave

I hadn't even thought about finding Mr. Right since Mom died and I moved back to my family home. I focused my time and energy on caring for Dad and grieving for Mom. Work would have to wait. My boss allowed me to take a leave of absence until I was ready.

At first, overseeing Dad's care had felt good, gave my life purpose. I didn't stop to question how I'd be able to care for him and work full-time, didn't consider how my move would affect my chance of adopting a child. I'd simply moved in without giving the situation much thought. Dad needed me. Besides, Baldwin loved the huge backyard.

* * *

After spending more than a month figuring out my new life, the time came to get back to work. I braved the traffic one Monday morning and headed to the office in Santa Monica. When I got there, a stranger was sitting at my desk.

"We didn't think you'd come back with your dad's illness and all," my supervisor, Abby, said. "Let's talk in my office."

I followed Abby to her plush office, complete with a huge fish tank. She sat behind her desk and motioned for me to take a seat in front of her floor-to-ceiling window.

"I'm sorry to tell you, but we hired someone new to take over your accounts," she said with concern in her voice.

That was when I noticed a hawk circling outside her window, close enough to touch. He looked huge with his red tail and scary-looking talons. When the hawk dived toward the window, I jumped.

"There's a hawk. Look."

Abby glanced out her window, unfazed. I took in the bird's large, hooked beak, like a dagger, and thought, *Maybe he's here to help me though this uncomfortable situation.*

"We only have a part-time support position open right now," Abby said with a wavering smile.

I watched the hawk fly off, free to roam the sky. Me? I sat there, listening, determined not to become prey.

"Part-time? Support position? No way," I said. "I have more than twenty years of experience."

"All I can offer you right now is a junior account executive position," she said. "We'll adjust your salary, of course, to match that position."

I got my full salary during my absence. Now that I'm back, they're going to cut my paycheck?

"Abby, I haven't worked as a junior account executive for years," I explained. "I want my vice president position back."

"That's not available."

"You can't demote someone for taking time off when their mom dies."

"Be patient," she said, picking up a pen. "We've got new business coming. We'll promote you back to VP when you get your own accounts again."

"Where am I supposed to work? There's a new person at my desk."

"You'll have to set up in the break room for now," she said. "I'll have a computer set up for you later today. Now, I've got to get ready for a meeting."

I walked out of her office, stunned. At least I had spoken up for myself. A baby step for sure, but still, a step. I tried to be grateful that I still had a job, but inputting info into spreadsheets made me want to scream. After one afternoon, I'd had enough. I banged my head on my makeshift desk in frustration.

Is this stupid job worth it? I'd rather be spending time with Baldwin.

Over the years, I'd seen other peers get pushed out at the agency, especially those going through a difficult time in their private lives. The latest had gotten the boot in the middle of a nasty divorce. I wouldn't allow them to kick me out. There were other jobs out there. I needed to find one.

I got busy. Called everyone I knew, looking for freelance gigs. I found a great one writing press releases for a friend who had recently started her own PR firm. The best part was that I got to work from home.

I gave notice the next day, free to roam the sky like that hawk. That meant no more rush-hour traffic, no more spreadsheets, and time to do doggy things with Baldwin.

* * *

Having a dog from the herding group meant I needed to continue training him. We'd tried the sport of dog agility in his puppy class and he liked it. Now, it was time to see what my boy could do on a real obstacle course.

One warm spring evening, Baldwin and I met six other dogs and their owners on the grass in the back of a church, waiting for our beginners agility class to start.

Baldwin looking up at me during agility class. I love the way he is so focused on me, waiting to take off! (photograph by Jim Crawford).

"Baldwin, look at that."

We watched a border collie fly past us, taking jumps, tunnels, and the weave poles at full speed. The owner was a handsome man around my age.

"Think you'll be able to do that someday?"

Baldwin pulled at his leash as if to answer, *Yes.*

Me? I found myself thinking about Mr. Right again. Maybe I'd meet him in agility.

I focused my attention on the man who had completed that clean run with his border collie.

"How long did it take to teach your dog to do that?"

"We've been training for a couple of years now." He wiped the sweat off his brow just in time for another attractive man to join in our conversation.

"What a good boy," the other man said, petting the talented border collie. "Are you my good boy? Give Daddy a kiss."

Daddy? I'd thought the man who ran the agility course with the dog owned him.

I asked, "That's your dog?"

The two men kissed each other. It was just a peck, but it was on the lips.

Baldwin and I both learned to weave; him in agility, me in life (author's photograph).

34. *Learning to Weave*

I dropped the Mr. Right idea and focused solely on my dog. There were so many obstacles to conquer, and Baldwin's enthusiasm was contagious.

Ask anyone in the sport of agility, and they'd tell you the weave poles present the ultimate challenge. Dogs who master this obstacle move with precision through the poles as fast as possible. People said it reminded them of a slalom event when skiers weaved in and out of poles at top speed.

I never thought I could teach my dog to do something so challenging. But with the help of my coach, Kristen, I found out that I could as long as I started at the beginning, one pole at a time. As with all dog training, the key to Baldwin's success was patience.

Within six months, Baldwin mastered a beginners course, including the weave poles. I loved to sprint next to him and watch his little black ears flap when he soared over jumps, climbed the Λ-frame, and *ta da*, weaved.

I entered Baldwin into his first trial. My fear of taking tests threatened to ruin the experience, but Baldwin wouldn't have it. His eagerness helped me move past my fears.

The trial meant getting up at the crack of dawn to begin the hour-and-a-half drive up the coast to Santa Barbara. My adrenaline pumping, I couldn't wait to see my boy in action.

We got there in plenty of time. The trial was already underway with the dogs in the top excellent class competing. They zoomed around the course, making me dizzy.

"Look, Baldwin." I held him in my arms, pointing him toward the show ring. "That could be you one day."

He wiggled to get out there and show me what he could do.

"Don't you worry, mister; no pressure," I said. "I'll be happy to make it through our novice beginners course today."

"Put that dog away." My coach, Kristen, startled me.

"I didn't know you'd be here," I said.

"I'm at every trial," she said. "Where's his crate?"

She followed us to the back where I had set up his crate next to a folding chair for me.

"Dogs love their crates," she said.

When I placed him inside, Baldwin stared at me, and his sad eyes begged me to take him out. I resisted.

Kristen pulled me away and headed to the novice show ring where Baldwin and I would compete.

"This is your course," she said like a drill sergeant. "Own it. You'll

195

have to walk it first without Baldwin and get your strategy down. Picture yourself running it. See Baldwin flying over the jumps, going through the tunnel, and conquering the weaves. Can you see it?"

"I guess so."

"That's not the right answer." Kristen stood with her hands on her hips, like Mom used to do. "I asked, can you see it?"

"I can see it," I said.

"Now, attack it."

When the time came to take Baldwin out and get ready for our first ever competitive run, he wiggled, kissed me, and clawed at my leg as if we'd been separated for a million years.

"This is it, buddy. Let's have fun."

The judges called us to the start line. I motioned for Baldwin to sit while I removed his leash.

"Stay." I took a few steps forward.

"Go when ready," the ring steward said.

I gave Baldwin a nod, and we took off. I watched him sail over the first jump; he made a perfect landing in front of the tunnel. I pointed him to the A-frame; he climbed it in three long strides, took two more jumps to the teeter, and slammed it to the ground like a pro. He sat on the table and waited until I motioned for him to take off again. He ran as fast as he could across the dog walk, straight into the weaves, maneuvering through the poles with ease.

I got so excited that I forgot to point him to the final jump. I caught my mistake in time, turned him around, and watched him sail over it to victory.

We sat on the grass together and basked in our glory. I felt proud of my boy.

"Nice job," Kristen said. "He almost missed that last jump. Good recovery."

The judge announced the winners.

"In the novice sixteen-inch division, Baldwin gets first place."

What? I'd always been uncoordinated in sports, the last to be picked for a team, yet with Baldwin, we came in first place.

A year later, Baldwin became the number one Puli in Agility in the United States with me as his handler. We had accomplished this incredible feat together, without a man. I couldn't wait to see what else Baldwin and I could do together.

35

Dr. Baldwin

The time had come to see what my boy would do with a flock of sheep. After making a reservation, Baldwin and I headed to a ranch in Chatsworth, not far from home, to find out if he had the DNA to herd. When Baldwin caught a whiff of the barnyard, his eyes lit up. He began pawing at the door of my car as I parked.

The moment we got out of the car, Baldwin grabbed my pant leg, pulling me to move faster, as if he thought, *I gotta get those sheep!*

"Baldwin, slow down!"

That little ball of fluff didn't listen. He kept pulling me and yanked me so hard that I lost my balance, landing face-first in the dirt.

"Shit," I yelled.

"You okay?" A handsome guy appeared out of nowhere. He was dressed like a cowboy, complete with boots, a hat, jeans, and a plaid shirt.

He helped me up and took Baldwin's leash from me.

"I'm Larry," he said, twirling Baldwin's leash like a lasso.

Oh, great. What's the best way to meet someone? Fall in the dirt and scream at your dog, of course.

I tried to gain my composure, brushed the dirt off, and shook Larry's hand. "Nice to meet you."

In my mind, I thought, *Thanks, Baldwin. You just blew our chances of making this cowboy your daddy.*

"You wait outside the ring over

Baldwin running towards the camera. He was as strong as he was adorable! (photograph by Pam Marks, PawPrince Studios).

there with my wife, Marilyn." Larry walked in the opposite direction with Baldwin.

My heart deflated a bit when I heard the word *wife*.

Larry opened the gate, and four sheep ran to huddle in a corner. "We'll see what this little dude of yours can do."

My sweet little Puli took off and ran after the sheep like a pro. That black fluff ball circled the sheep to keep them together as a flock and then nipped at their heels to drive them forward to Larry. Baldwin moved his weight from one paw to the other and stared at the sheep with intensity before he took off again to drive them in the opposite direction.

Baldwin's confidence and know-how took my breath away. I'd thought he'd be scared of animals more than three times his size. But Baldwin showed no fear. To watch my dog work, see his DNA kick in, made me feel better.

Turned out, Marilyn did more than assist her husband in sheep-herding classes.

"Your dog would make an excellent therapy dog," she told me as we watched Baldwin circling the sheep.

"You think so? Isn't he a bit too wild?"

"Absolutely not," she said. "My dogs herd sheep and compete in agility, but when we enter the hospital, something happens. They calm down."

"I've always wanted to train a therapy dog."

"I'm a certified evaluator for Therapy Dogs International and have been taking my dogs to visit kids at County-USC for fifteen years. I can help you train him and get certified too."

"He definitely has the instinct," Larry said, bringing my dog back.

"And a great attitude," Marilyn added. "The kids will go nuts over this little guy."

No children of her own, Marilyn told me she'd decided not to cry about what she didn't have. Instead, she spent her time and energy helping children in need. I liked her immediately. Baldwin did too. With Marilyn's help, he passed the test with flying colors in a couple of months.

* * *

We joined Marilyn and her dogs, Shiloh and Mick, on their next visit to the hospital. I didn't know how, but my boy knew what to do the moment we arrived.

35. Dr. Baldwin

Groomed and dressed in his doctor's scrubs costume, Baldwin squealed when we entered the parking lot.

"Look, Marilyn. He knows where we're going."

"I told you that dog would be a natural therapy dog."

Baldwin wiggled his little stump of a tail, ready to get to work. He knew, and I knew he knew. Therapy work would become my sweet dog's life mission.

When we got out of the car, he headed straight toward the entrance. I didn't know how to get inside. How did he?

Baldwin couldn't contain himself. He greeted everyone on the elevator, wagging his stump of a tail. When the door opened, Baldwin made a beeline to Leita, the head of the children's program.

"Who's this little doctor?"

Leita reached down to pet Baldwin, but he gave her his paw to shake instead.

"Oh, a formal hello," she said. "This must be Baldwin."

"He's ready to work."

"Good. Marilyn, I want you and your dogs to go room to room today, and we'll have Dr. Baldwin visit a special little girl who's waiting in the playroom."

Turned out, Maria was recovering from a round of chemo she had earlier that day, so she couldn't be around any other kids because of vulnerability to germs. The seven-year-old looked gaunt and tired, her complexion pale, almost transparent. With a frame so thin from her treatments, her cheekbones stood out, and her eyes sunk in.

Maria's mother sat next to her and held her daughter's fragile little hand. The young cancer patient looked like a mannequin. She didn't move, just sat there quietly, a blank stare on her face. When Maria saw Baldwin, she took a deep breath and laughed out loud at my Muppet dog, which brought some color back into her face.

I asked Maria in my broken Spanish if she wanted Baldwin to sit next to her. Before she answered, Baldwin hopped on the couch and stretched his entire body across her lap. She rubbed under his chin, and he sighed, putting his head down, and then closed his eyes. Maria breathed deep with him, and she looked better, healthier, with every inhale.

Baldwin spent an hour in that playroom. Maria stroked him, her hands moving over him in rhythm, like someone praying the rosary.

I couldn't help but think about the prayer, Hail Mary, Full of Grace. I was witnessing a miracle. This high-energy dog who ran agility

199

courses, herded sheep, and played ball for hours was lying still, doing exactly what this little girl needed. I thanked God for showing me grace in action, mercy, awe, gratitude, and unconditional love, all wrapped up in my little black dog. At that moment, I realized life is a gift.

Maybe if I was more trustful, like Maria, Baldwin's grace could help me too and be the key to finding love. In the meantime, my dog and I would continue to live life and enjoy each minute, each hour, each day together.

36

September Mourning

"Darling, I'm coming back to LA next Tuesday," Angel said. She lived at Cape Cod now, returning to Los Angeles several times a year to see her kids and her friends. "Presley has a gig in Hollywood. You must come."

"Wouldn't miss it for the world."

I'd watched Presley perform many times while she was in high school. She was a talented little lady, and I couldn't wait to see her all grown up, performing in a club.

Baldwin makes everyone laugh in his red hat, jumping through a hoop during agility class (photograph by Caryn Levy).

I'm Not Single, I Have a Dog

"My flight lands in the afternoon," she said. "We can meet at the Troubadour."

"Can't wait to see you! Will your new beau be with you?"

"Not this time, but you'll get to meet him this Thanksgiving when you visit us." The two of them split their time between the Cape and Jamaica.

I couldn't wait to meet Coot. Angel was lucky to have found love for the second time. She deserved it. Fate brought Angel and her Jamaican boyfriend together when she was on vacation. They didn't spend hours online searching for each other or endure dreadful blind dates. Angel didn't waste her time doing all the things I had done to find love.

Me? I was through with wasting my time looking for love. I was instead choosing to live my life to the fullest with or without a man. If I met someone along the way, great. If I didn't, at least I'd be doing what made me happy.

I knew I loved participating in dog sports with Baldwin and visiting kids at the hospital. The last time Angel had been in town, she'd joined us.

"What do the kids need?" she asked.

"Art supplies," I answered.

"I can do art supplies."

And she did.

When I picked her up the day of the visit, she'd bought so much stuff that I could barely fit it all in my car.

* * *

The next morning, I woke to the sound of a rooster crowing from a neighbor's backyard. I stayed in bed for a while, breathing in a feeling of peace. For the first time in forever, I felt satisfied with my life, no longer needing a man to feel complete. At forty-three, I actually appreciated my single status, although the feeling of being an old maid did creep up on me from time to time.

My dream, from the night before, was so vivid that I could recall every detail.

It started in the backyard of my family home in the San Fernando Valley in the suburbs of Los Angeles. I saw myself throwing the ball for Baldwin until our fun was interrupted by someone who leaned on the car horn out front. Baldwin and I went to investigate.

The honking came from the driver of a car Angel had sent to pick Baldwin and me up. I couldn't wait to see my friend who'd been living in Jamaica and Cape Cod since the death of her husband nine years earlier.

202

36. September Mourning

I jumped into the car with my dog and remembered a conversation I'd had with Angel about her perfect future—to grow old, surrounded by family and friends. Angel wanted to build an oasis for all the people she loved, including me. She envisioned an adobe home shaped in a half-circle, with everyone having their own room, and a common kitchen area in the middle. I knew that was where we were headed.

I felt a sense of excitement when the car pulled into our destination—Angel's oasis. We arrived at sunset with reds, purples, golds, brilliant hues of aqua and green combining as the perfect backdrop. The car stopped in front of a building that looked exactly like I'd imagined, just like Angel had wished for, framed by snowcapped mountains in the distance.

Wildflowers grew around the structure among the brittlebush sprinkled with purple lupine. A hard dirt path led straight to the front door.

"The only thing that could make this picture more perfect would be Angel and maybe a rainbow."

Poof! A rainbow appeared.

But no Angel. Birds chirped, and bunnies with their little white cottontails hopped around the grounds. It was a wonder that Baldwin didn't try to herd them. Instead, he stayed right by my side.

The scent of roses greeted us, although I didn't see any rose bushes nearby.

"Angel's here somewhere. She always wears rose perfume. Angel, it's your sweetikins. Where are you?"

I couldn't find her, but I knew where to locate my room. We headed upstairs—me in the lead, Baldwin at my heels. When I opened the door, I caught my breath.

Natural light lit up a plush bed in the center of the room. Baldwin jumped up and rolled around on the lush sheets and blankets like Snoopy. Angel had decorated in my favorite colors—pale blues, earthy browns— with a floral print Ralph Lauren comforter.

The best part of the room? The ceiling made of glass so that I could fall asleep, counting stars.

The moment I jumped on the bed next to Baldwin, a shooting star raced across the sky.

"I have nothing more to wish for. Angel's thought of everything I could ever want."

I wanted to spend more time asleep in Angel's oasis. But I couldn't escape to dreamland while the gardener mowed the front lawn outside my bedroom window. *Time to get my butt out of bed.*

I'm Not Single, I Have a Dog

Still in my pajamas, I stopped in front of Dad's television on the way to take Baldwin outside. A plane had just crashed into the World Trade Center, and the news ran the footage over and over again.

I thought, *I'm so glad I don't know anyone who's flying today.*

But I did. Angel's flight from Boston had left that morning.

A wall of denial kept Angel safe—at least in my mind.

I went on with my day, played ball with Baldwin, fed him, took a shower, brushed my teeth, got busy in my home office, made phone calls, and answered emails. Baldwin hopped in the car with me, and we headed to Starbucks for my morning coffee fix.

"Did you hear what happened?" the barista asked. He looked shaken, as though he'd lost his best friend.

"You mean the plane crash?"

"Not one crash. Two planes deliberately flew into the World Trade Center. They're talking terrorism," he said.

Everything slowed down, and his words stabbed my denial open. I couldn't hide from the truth any longer.

Angel. No. She couldn't have been on one of those planes.

I drove home as fast as possible. Baldwin and I ran into the house like Olympic sprinters, straight to the den to get the latest from CNN. I stood by Dad, too nervous to sit. We watched two planes hit the towers. The video kept repeating, and neither of us said a word.

The explosions were followed by trails of heavy black smoke with red flames shooting into the sky where the towers had once stood. Crowds of people ran through the streets of Manhattan, covered in ash, terrified, injured, and bleeding.

Then, the newscaster said, "The first plane originated from Boston."

That's when reality hit me. The room swirled out of control, and the walls closed in on me.

That's the Baldwin face that I fell madly in love with! To me, he looks like Cookie Monster only Baldwin is black (photograph by Jim Crawford).

204

"Angel was on that plane." My knees buckled, and I grabbed Dad for support.

"Oh, Suzie, I'm sorry. Not your friend Angel. The one with the little Scottie dog?"

He put his arms around me and let me cry on his shoulder. I tried to stop the tears by breathing deep, but panic flooded me. I shuddered. I couldn't stop shaking as adrenaline rushed my bloodstream. My legs could no longer hold me, so I eased myself to the floor. Baldwin lay across my lap to steady me.

Angel. My incredible friend and confidante who had protected, comforted, and inspired me for the last twenty years. Angel, who had lived her life with pure love. How could I live without her?

Angel perished that morning on American Airlines Flight 11, along with all the other passengers and crew members. I would never again see Angel on this earth.

Then I remembered the dream, so vivid and real; it evoked all my senses, even my sense of smell.

What did it mean?

I flashed on a Bible verse—John 14:2. *In My Father's house are many rooms. The scripture goes on to say, If it were not so, would I have told you that I go to prepare a place for you?*

Had Angel shown me a slice of heaven?

37

A Good-Bye Tale

While the world grieved for the 2,606 people who had died at the World Trade Center, I tried to wrap my head around a world without Angel. Not possible.

Hundreds of Angel's friends; her daughters Presley and Percy; and other family members gathered at a mansion in the Hollywood Hills, the estate donated for Angel's memorial service. More people would have come, including her mother who lived in England, but the world's planes were grounded after 9/11. Those who could make it on that hot Southern California day congregated outside, gathered on the lawn to remember the woman who had touched the lives of everyone she met.

A Catholic priest began the service. I couldn't concentrate on anything he said until he introduced Angel's youngest daughter. Hiding behind dark sunglasses, Percy carried her guitar to face the crowd. She sang one of Angel's favorites—Leonard Cohen's "Hallelujah."

The crowd sat silent while Percy, without breaking down, sang the touching words of Cohen's song about love and loss. The music chilled me in the hot sunlight. I cried so hard that my nose stuffed up and stayed that way for days.

Presley, her firstborn daughter, also made the mourners gathered that day weep. She shared a letter Angel had written at the time of her birth.

"She gave me this letter on my sixteenth birthday," Presley said, her eyes filled with tears. "*Welcome to the world, little one,*" she began. "*You are the best thing that has ever happened to me. I loved every moment of my pregnancy. Your dad did too. He managed to gain weight right along with me. We shared our hopes and dreams about you, excited to witness every moment of your youth. I wanted to give you as much love as you have given me. Just remember, life is filled with good times and bad ones. Cherish the good ones and learn from your mistakes. No matter what life brings you, just know that I am always there for you and that I will always love you. Love, Mom."*

When the priest asked if anyone wanted to share a memory, I raised my hand first. My inspiration? Brave Presley and Percy. I had to honor my friend.

I walked slowly to the microphone, breathing deep to steady my nerves. When I reached the front of the crowd and looked out over all the gloomy faces, I knew I had to pull myself together for Angel.

"This is a story about the last time I saw my dear friend Angel," I said, my voice shaky. "When she found out about my pup, Baldwin, being certified as a therapy dog, she immediately wanted to help. Turned out, we were due to visit the kids at County-USC while she was in town. She said, 'Darling, let me go with you. What can I bring?' I told her the kids needed art supplies."

I stopped for a moment to pull myself together.

"When I picked her up the day of the visit, Angel came outside with boxes of art materials for the kids. She had everything—crayons, markers, paper, paint, you name it."

I paused again, took a deep breath.

"That day, Angel blessed all the children. I feel lucky to have been blessed by knowing Angel, a true angel here on Earth."

At the end of the service, I looked up at a stately oak tree on the grounds. At the very top, the leaves rustled and fell to the ground like tears. I didn't feel any wind; everything else in the backyard stayed perfectly still. Only the top part of the tree moved in the invisible breeze, as if Mother Nature were grieving along with us.

Now, Angel and John would rest in peace together.

* * *

After months of no communication, Jack called. "I heard about Angel."

My heart lifted at the sound of his voice. Not that I wanted to get back together with him. But still, we had history, and I missed him. While we had been a couple, he'd spent time with Angel, and he knew how much she meant to me.

"I'm going to Ground Zero to help in the cleanup efforts," Jack told me.

Neither of us understood the gravity of the situation of post–9/11 Manhattan, both in shock over the attack on the country and the loss of my friend.

"Look for Angel's gold ring," I told him. "You know, the one with the cross on it. If you find it, keep it for the girls."

Jack flew to New York, but he couldn't volunteer to help. In fact, no one could. The disaster and ensuing fires released thousands of tons of matter into the atmosphere, much of it toxic. Jack couldn't even get close to Ground Zero.

* * *

Months later, Jack phoned me. "Did you see the current issue of *People* magazine?"

"No. Why?"

"There's a story about the items found in the 9/11 rubble. They found Angel's gold ring, the one with the cross, the one you told me to look for."

"You've got to be kidding me. They found her ring?"

"It's a message from Angel," he said. "She's letting her loved ones know that she's at peace."

To this day, I am still amazed that the ring hadn't disintegrated in the explosion.

* * *

That Thanksgiving, I flew to New York because I had to see Ground Zero for myself. The area surrounding the place where the Twin Towers had once stood was still a major disaster area. Broken glass, blown out from nearby storefronts, was scattered all over. Everything was still covered with ash. The smell of fire and oily smoke was overwhelming. A never-ending sea of notes, letters, and photos covered the fencing that surrounded the deep hole.

I felt bad because I hadn't made a sign or thought to bring anything to add to the memorial to honor Angel. None of the nearby stores were open to buy anything. There was only a coffee vendor on the corner. I ordered a cup of coffee made the exact way Angel had liked hers. Angel had so loved her coffee. I set the paper cup on the sidewalk near the barriers around the deep black pit.

I stood there along with hundreds of others who had come to pay their respects. The noise of the crowds faded when I thanked Angel for being such a good friend to me.

"Your sweetikins misses you. You will live in my heart forever. Rest in peace, my darling friend. Rest in peace."

38

Sleeps with Dogs

Three major deaths in three years. That'd make anyone's head spin. I made another emergency session with Beverly.

"Angel's girls lost their dad nine years ago and now their mom," I said. "Kids are supposed to live longer than their parents—that's the natural order of things—but not when you're a teenager or in your early twenties. I don't know how to help them."

"Being there for them helps. Listening helps," Beverly said, handing me the Kleenex box once again. "Loss comes to everyone at some point; nobody walks alone. That can be a great comfort to them and to you too."

"When Blondie died, I tried my best to find her reincarnated doggie soul. With Mom, I slept my life away for way too long. But Angel's death gives me nightmares. Even sleep doesn't comfort me."

"When a death is violent like Angel's, it can take a long time to accept. Be easy on yourself. Your emotions might be intense, but that's normal."

"I can't let myself fall into that dark pit of despair again. After Mom died, it took me a long time to come back to life."

"Losing your mother is a primal hit. It's natural to feel consumed by pain, fear, and sadness at the loss of such a significant influence in your life."

"I know Mom died peacefully in her sleep. Not Angel. Her death makes me want to scream."

"You're not alone. We all experienced a loss of safety that day, a loss of trust, and above all, a loss of innocence. You have to deal with all that *and* the loss of your friend."

"I can't stop thinking about Angel's last moments. The terrorists made the passengers huddle in the back of the plane. Did she know they were going to crash?"

"Freud would call that feeling the painful bit by bit process of letting go. Grief involves a process of review and relinquishment. That's what your thoughts are about. Don't stop them, and don't act on them, just let them be."

"My friends must be sick of hearing me talk about death."

"Grief is a process. Make time every day to express your grief and then pull yourself together and get on with the business of living."

"I'm afraid to do things that never used to bother me, like getting on an airplane. But I have to get over my fears quick. I have a business trip later this week to Vegas."

"I understand; everyone's on edge right now. Many of my clients who suffer from a fear of flying had to learn how to parent themselves. When feelings of fear come up, let them go, take slow and deep breaths, and try to relax."

"I don't want to live in fear. I want my life back. I want Angel back."

"The best way to honor Angel, your mom, and Blondie is to fully *live* yourself."

"That's what Angel would want me to do; that's what I've been trying to do. I went to a dinner party the other night."

"Good for you."

"Met this guy, Simon. He seemed full of himself, but I gave him my number anyway. He's completely different from any of the other guys I've dated. That's a good sign."

"Yes, it is. I've been telling you to date outside your comfort zone and make changes to attract a healthier partner. Look how healthy you've become."

* * *

Beverly's counsel didn't help me from dreading my business trip to Las Vegas. A short flight, but still, I had no idea what to expect.

The first thing I saw when I arrived at LAX—officers with their guns. They were everywhere. I joined the mix of travelers who were figuring out the new airport rituals. At a security checkpoint, I had to take off my shoes and take out my laptop and then wait in a long line for an agent to wave me through the metal detector.

I sat at my gate, took a deep breath, tried to calm myself like Beverly suggested. The thought of sitting on that plane made my chest tighten.

My cell phone rang, and the ring startled me. I rummaged through my purse, my hands clammy, but managed to find my phone in time.

"Hello there," Simon said. "How's business?"

"I wondered if you'd call." Hearing from Simon calmed my nerves, as it was a diversion. "I'm at the airport, my first flight since 9/11."

"Good for you, darling."

He used the word *darling*, just like Angel. Maybe that was a sign. Maybe Angel had sent him to me.

The conversation was easy. We discussed work and my sweet boy Baldwin. He told me he was raising three kids on his own. I found myself so engaged in our conversation that I didn't notice the door to the plane close. We talked until a flight attendant asked me to hang up and prepare for departure.

He called me back the moment my plane landed.

"How'd you know we landed?"

"I checked with the airline."

I didn't remember sharing my flight details with him. We talked while I waited for my luggage at baggage claim and continued as I grabbed a taxi. I knew I had to get right to work once I got to the resort, but our conversation was going so well I didn't want to stop. I liked this guy. But before I got in too deep, I had to find out what he thought about dogs.

"I have to ask you something," I said.

"Ask me."

"This might be a deal-breaker. How do you feel about dogs?"

"I love dogs," he said. "In fact, I have two rescue mutts of my own."

"Really?" That was a good sign. "I have this amazing dog who sleeps in bed with me."

"Of course you do," he said in his sexy British accent. "He's your baby."

The stars aligned, and the angels sang from heaven above. Simon might be everything I'd been looking for. But for now, it was off to work for me.

* * *

I couldn't wait to see Simon when I returned later that week. But we had a difficult time syncing our schedules. He called several times a day and sent thoughtful emails, making me feel comfortable, like we were already a couple. Maybe this relationship would work. At least we were taking things slowly.

We finally found an evening that worked for both of us. He wanted to make me dinner at his house. I couldn't wait.

Before I could get through his front door, Simon grabbed me and kissed me.

"Hello to you too," I said.

"You look lovely, darling. Welcome to Chez Simon. Let me show you around."

His house was immaculate, not a speck of dust anywhere, and it reminded me of clean-freak Bobby. I considered myself tidy, but my home never looked that clean, not with an ailing father and an active dog to care for.

"Where are your kids?"

"They're with their mother; we share custody."

He had told me he raised his kids on his own but hadn't said anything about their mother. I'd thought perhaps Simon might be a widower.

"You were married?"

"For seven years. She left me a year ago."

Wonder what happened. Takes a lot to drive a mother from her kids.

"Where're your dogs?"

"They're outside. I don't allow them in the house."

I couldn't avoid seeing the red flags waving in front of my face this time. Something about Simon didn't seem right.

"I thought you understood that I sleep with my dog. He goes everywhere with me."

"I do understand, but you won't be able to sleep with him at my house. I have a rule: dogs stay outside."

"Look, I really appreciate all your efforts to make me this lovely dinner, but that rule doesn't work for me."

"You're not one of those women who chooses her dog over a relationship, are you?"

"Actually, I am one of those women. And proud of it."

I left. I'd learned my lesson, and there were too many red flags already showing up. He didn't seem to care.

I never did hear back from him. That was when I decided staying single might be the best lifestyle for me. I already enjoyed a full life with Baldwin, my work, and my friends. Why would I do anything to mess that up?

39

Ashes to Ashes

"Thanks to you, Baldwin, I avoided another future heartache."

I felt empowered when I returned that night. Baldwin greeted me by bouncing off the walls. I grabbed him mid-bounce to hug him tight.

"My gut told me to get away from that sexy Brit, and this time, I listened."

To celebrate my newfound enlightenment when it came to relationships, I turned on the stereo and danced with Baldwin.

Dogs are better companions then men," I belted out. "*They'll never judge you and will love you just the way you are. They're a lot easier to train and are always down to snuggle. Dogs don't complain or tell you you're crazy. They're always excited to see you, never play mind games, and put their humans first.*"

While I glided across the living room floor, dipping and swinging my pup in celebration, I realized, "That asshole lied to me. He wasn't raising his kids by himself. He didn't even love his dogs enough to let them inside."

"I'm no longer on the hunt for a man to fill in my missing pieces."

My heart filled with gratefulness for Baldwin and my remarkable friendships.

* * *

"Don't worry, boy," I told Baldwin the next morning. "We're going on your favorite hike later today, like I promised. Let me finish my oatmeal and get some work done first."

Seemed like he understood. He wagged his little stump of a tail and then curled up at my feet to wait, Dad's CNN blasting away in the den. Right there at the kitchen table, I had a revelation.

"I don't need a man to be happy and fulfilled. So what? I never got married. Big deal. Never had kids. Too bad. Never bought that family home with the white picket fence I'd dreamed about. Boohoo."

Baldwin sat up and wagged his tail in agreement.

I'm Not Single, I Have a Dog

"I'm satisfied to be an independent, single woman. I've got a good job, terrific friends, and another dog to love. My life with you, Baldwin, is quite the journey. You've opened up a whole new world filled with dog competitions, visiting kids in the hospital, and lots of wet kisses. I might not lead the typical life but what a life I've lived."

Baldwin barked three times, which to me sounded like a *Yes!*

"What more do I need? You don't drink, you never play those stupid mind games, and I don't have to save money to put you through college. You're authentic, you're consistent, and you've taught me to live in the moment."

When I finished my oatmeal, Baldwin pulled at the hem of my slacks and led me outside to play ball.

"How could I feel depressed when I look at a face like yours? You couldn't care less if I put on a few pounds. You never worry about money or get upset over bad hair days—yours or mine. Your only interest is love. Oh wait, let's see. Maybe this ball too."

Baldwin ran after the ball as fast as he could.

"We've got to do something to mark my epiphany. Time to let go of Blondie's ashes. You with me?"

Gold canister in hand, I leashed Baldwin and headed to one of our favorite hikes in the San Fernando Valley. Aliso Canyon snaked through a beautiful area shaded by tall pine trees. The goal was to make it to a small stream at the top. The moment we stepped onto that dirt path, I relaxed. The grief I'd been carrying around since Blondie died dissipated.

I'd lived in fear, afraid of what would or wouldn't happen next. Instead of getting all charged up about how a situation might or might not turn out, I noticed I felt fine, not knowing. Time to allow my life to bloom.

Baldwin in the backyard of the Northridge House (photograph by Jim Crawford).

39. Ashes to Ashes

I thought about my pound dog, Blondie, and everything we'd been through together. I remembered the time I had taken her to see the California poppies that bloomed each spring. How beautiful she'd looked, running in a sea of yellow and orange poppies—a flower celebrated for its strength in bright colors and spirit, like my dog, like me.

My thoughts returned to Baldwin, the black fluff ball Mom had bought me before she died. Thanks to her, I got a hint of how it felt to be a mother when I dropped him off at doggie daycare. I couldn't believe I'd cried when I left him there.

Baldwin ran ahead, but I didn't get nervous. I knew where to find him on that hot day—in the stream at the top of the canyon.

Under the shade of a Monterey pine, I rested on one of the giant boulders that rose up out of the stream, pressed my lips to the gold canister with Blondie's remains, and felt the peace, the quiet, in this beautiful canyon. Baldwin dashed in and out of the water, and I opened the canister.

I grabbed a handful of Blondie's ashes, letting them filter though my fingers. A gentle breeze like the one at Angel's memorial service carried them up in the air. The ashes danced in the rays of sunlight like butterflies and then fell in graceful arcs on the water.

"Angel's here with us, Baldwin."

I took another handful of Blondie's ashes and let them sail through the air and float into the water, making ripples on the surface.

I turned the entire canister over to let Blondie's ashes float away. I imagined them taking all my broken relationships with them. Gone, all gone.

The one thing all these men had in common? Me. I'd chosen them. Clearly, I wasn't good at choosing a man for a lifelong partner.

I watched Baldwin play in the water, so alive, so in the moment. I realized that choosing canine companions and dear friends came easy to me.

I stood for one last look at Blondie's final resting place, Baldwin by my side, gold canister now empty. What if my pound mutt, Blondie, appeared? Would she impart some ancient wisdom from the other side? In my mind, I saw her standing on that rock and heard her voice in my heart. I knew now that she was a part of me, like Angel, right there inside my heart.

I heard Blondie's words, *You're right; I've found lots of turkey in heaven.*

Afterword

I've made it to my sixties without getting married or having children—unless you count my dogs. So I guess one could say I'm officially an old maid, a spinster—my biggest fear. But I'm not afraid or embarrassed anymore. I'm here to tell you that being single is not a bad thing. I've grown to appreciate my independence, and I have no plans to give it up. I definitely don't feel alone or lonely. In fact, an uncluttered, single lifestyle works for me. I appreciate both the solitude and spending time with my many friends, both two- and four-legged.

So much has changed. I look older, my metabolism went south, I made it through the great recession of 2007, and I injured one of my big toes when I tumbled into a five-foot hole while walking my current pack. Falling into a hole messed up my left foot, but my aches and pains don't keep me from playing with my dogs.

I've had my share of challenges, but the search, the dream of finding Mr. Right is no longer one of them. I feel a sense of relief that the obsession to get married faded away the morning I realized I have much to appreciate. Took me years of therapy, but I've finally started counting the many blessings I do have.

Besides, I believe it's better to be single than devote yourself to the wrong person. Being alone doesn't mean you're lonely. Quite the contrary. I love spending time with my four-legged family members—no drama, no arguments, only unconditional love.

There are many ways to create a family. Like I learned from Beverly, life is filled with choices. Nobody has to wait as long as I did to start making the right ones. Begin by loving yourself.

I learned to love myself enough to take care of the abortion I had so long ago. When I joined Angel's church, one of the ministers actually opened up the sanctuary for me and performed a funeral service for my unborn child. I still think about the baby I could have had but it no longer guts me like it did before.

It was the #MeToo movement that allowed me to admit I'd been raped by Bobby. I held that secret for so long. It was such a terrifying and confusing time that it took me more than twenty-five years to come to terms with the truth.

Remember the family house in Northridge? I bought it from my sister, Erin, and my brother, Will, after Dad died. I felt proud to be a homeowner, but the thrill didn't last long. I joined the many homeowners who lost their houses during the recession. I'd unwittingly signed a fraudulent loan. At the time, my gut screamed, *Don't sign!* But I didn't listen. Instead, I learned an expensive lesson that Angel tried to teach me so long ago: always listen to your gut.

That experience solidified my belief that everything happens for a reason. I had to be forced out of that house before I could sort through and get rid of fifty years of family stuff. I needed that kick in the pants. Difficult to say good-bye to that place of so many memories. But today, I'm glad I left.

Once I let go, I discovered the perfect home for my canine family and me. Every morning, I wake up and feel grateful for my small house, located a block from a dog-friendly beach.

I love everything about the place. The people are laid-back and friendly, I see seals and dolphins jumping and playing in the Pacific, and the weather's always perfect because, as the saying goes, *there's no bad weather on the beach.* To top it off, I've met some amazing dogs. And their people.

My beach house represents another important lesson I learned from Beverly: miracles can happen when you let go. Everything fell into place when I stopped fighting my circumstances. See what happens when you let go?

My present dog family consists of two fur children, both stunning Australian shepherds—five-year-old Seven and my four-month-old puppy Paige Turner.

I am living one of my dreams, thanks to Michelle Zahn and LePaws dog talent agency. Seven and Paige are professional actors. I trained them and work as their trainer on set. In fact, the two of them just worked a print ad last week. One of my favorite jobs happened before I brought Paige into our lives. Seven got booked on a show starring Mike Tyson. During dress rehearsal, I walked Seven on set and the audience went crazy with ohhs and ahhs. I got goosebumps.... I had finally made it. Besides, the heavyweight champion boxer told me I owned the best-looking dog he'd ever seen. I agree.

Seven continues Baldwin's legacy and works as a therapy dog. Paige

This is me today with my current pack, Paige Turner, left, and Seven (photograph by Pam Marks, PawPrince Studios).

will, too, as soon as she's old enough. I also volunteer my time evaluating other dogs and their owners who want to become therapy dog teams for Therapy Dogs International. I figure the more dog love I can help spread around the planet, the better the world we live in becomes.

I work from home these days in order to spend the majority of my time with Seven and Paige Turner. We stay active, explore hiking trails, swim at the beach, and play ball together. Their deep love and devotion reminds me of Baldwin, who supported me with his special kind of love through so many deaths.

I still suffer from the occasional panic attack, but with the help of my good friends, cuddles from my dogs, and the knowledge that this too shall pass, I find my way back to a positive outlook. Sometimes, all I need to do is take Seven and Paige Turner on a walk to gain a different perspective.

Years ago, I became a Universal Life Church minister. So far, I've performed weddings for two couples, and I've baptized one child—another goddaughter, Lindsay. I've also used my clergy status to baptize countless dogs, including my own.

Jack and I maintained a good friendship after he finally moved out. Jack turned out to be an excellent friend. I wonder what would've happened if I'd come to that realization earlier, if I hadn't allowed him to live off of me for so long. Took me all that time to comprehend that no one can make another person change. Once again, I needed to let go.

During the writing of this memoir, Jack, the man I'd spent ten years of my life with, took his own life. He'd experienced a traumatic brain injury after he got hit by the car so long ago. Doctors credited Jack's meditation practice for keeping the symptoms at bay. But Jack's demons finally caught up with him. During his final years, he suffered too much, mentally and physically, and tried everything he could to get better. But in the end, nothing helped. May Jack, my friend, rest in peace.

I think of Angel often, especially when I feel a gentle breeze on my face. How I miss my dear friend.

I've developed a relationship with my mom from beyond the grave. Beverly said it could be done. Now, I believe her.

Index